Books by Don L. Gates

Teaching a Learner Driver -
A guide for amateur instructors

The Driving Test & How to Pass -
An examiner's guide to the 'L' test

How to Drive on a Motorway

Driving at Night & in Bad Weather

Teaching a Learner Driver

A GUIDE FOR AMATEUR INSTRUCTORS

Don L. Gates

TEACHING A LEARNER DRIVER

A GUIDE FOR AMATEUR INSTRUCTORS

1st edition copyright © 1994 Don L. Gates
2nd edition copyright © 2011 Don L. Gates
3rd edition copyright © 2018 Don L. Gates
4th edition copyright © 2019 Don L. Gates

All rights reserved. No part of this book may be reproduced, or stored in a retrieval system, or transmitted in any form or by any means, electronic, mechanical, photocopying, recording, or otherwise, without express written permission of the publisher.

Contents

INTRODUCTION 8

1 PREPARATIONS 10
DRIVING SCHOOLS 12
YOU, THE INSTRUCTOR 15
THE TRAINING VEHICLE 17

2 THE FIRST LESSON 23
THE COCKPIT DRILL 26
THE CONTROLS LESSON 28
Accelerator 29
Footbrake 30
Clutch 31
Steering Wheel 33
Handbrake (Parking Brake) 34
The Gear Lever 35
Indicators 37
The Horn 38
Other Controls 39
STARTING THE ENGINE 40
FINDING THE BITING POINT 42
MOVING OFF AND STOPPING 45
Practising Moving off and Stopping 49
Angle Starts and Hill Starts 49
CHANGING GEARS 51

Changing Up 51

Changing Down 54

GENERAL ADVICE 57

ENDING THE LESSON 60

THE FOLLOWING LESSON... 61

3 APPROACHING JUNCTIONS 62
CLUTCH CONTROL 62

TURNING LEFT 64

Turning Left into a Side Road.. 65

Turning Left onto a Major Road.. 68

Variations in the routine 70

Practising Left Turns 71

INSTRUCTION ON THE MOVE 72

Left into a Side Road.. 72

Left onto a Major Road.. 73

EMERGING AT JUNCTIONS.. 75

TURNING RIGHT 76

Turning Right onto a Major Road 77

Turning Right into a Side Road 81

Practising Right Turns 85

INSTRUCTION ON THE MOVE 86

Right onto a Major Road 86

Right into a Minor Road 87

STEERING FAULTS 89

THE NEXT STAGE OF JUNCTION PRACTISE........................ 90

CROSSROADS 94

ROUNDABOUTS 96
Turning Left at a Roundabout 100
Taking the Road Ahead 101
Turning Right at a Roundabout 102
Practising Roundabouts 105
MINI ROUNDABOUTS 110
Signals 110
Steering 110

4 THE EXERCISES 111
HILL STARTS 111
Practising Hill Starts 113
ANGLE STARTS 115
Practising Angle Starts 116
THE EMERGENCY STOP 118
Practising the Emergency Stop 121
REVERSING 124
Practising Straight Reversing 127
Left Hand Reverse 130
Reversing Practise 131
TURNING IN THE ROAD 137
Practising the Turn 141
CLUTCH CONTROL EXERCISE ON A GRADIENT 144
REVERSING AROUND SHARP CORNERS 146
Practising the Sharp Reverse 148
REVERSING TO THE RIGHT 149
Practising the Right Hand Reverse 150

PARKING 153
Reversing Into a Bay 153
Reverse Bay Parking Practise 154
Reversing Out of a Bay 156
Parallel Parking 157
Parallel Parking Practise 160

5 DEALING WITH TRAFFIC 162
TRAFFIC LIGHTS 169
PEDESTRIAN CROSSINGS 174
DUAL CARRIAGEWAYS.. 175
INTERSECTIONS 178
DUAL CARRIAGEWAYS AND THE NATIONAL SPEED LIMIT 184
ANIMALS, CHILDREN AND THE LEARNER 187
MAJOR CROSSROADS 188
Offside Turning.. 189
Nearside Turning 190

6 PLANNING A LESSON PROGRAMME 195

7 DEVELOPING RESPONSIBILITY 202

INTRODUCTION

Many years ago, a sister of mine expressed an interest in learning to drive and being a keen driver myself I offered to teach her... what a carry on! We started off in the large car park of a famous furniture manufacturer, full of good intentions, but it wasn't until she was in the driving seat that I realised I didn't have a clue where to start. Needless to say, the venture was not very successful.

Some years later I became a professional driving instructor and, when I decided to start up my own driving school, the family came to me for lessons. Things went according to plan this time because in the meantime someone had taught me how to teach.

If you're thinking of teaching somebody to drive, this is the book you need. It's written by a professional who works with learner drivers every day of his working life. With over thirty five years of experience, both as a driving instructor and driving examiner, I will help you to train a learner driver to be safe, confident and capable. With the help of this book, you will learn how to structure lessons, and how do deliver driving instruction like a professional, avoiding many of the pitfalls that amateur teachers fall into.

The instructions are easy to follow and all tricky points are illustrated with clear diagrams. Everything is covered from gear changing, through to manoeuvring skills to preparation for the test.

With a careful study of this book, you'll really enjoy teaching the art of driving and improving your own skills; and, most importantly, your learner driver should pass first time!

1
PREPARATIONS

Throughout these pages I have taken a sometimes serious, but often light-hearted look at the task of teaching someone to drive. A sense of humour is essential if you are to succeed in this potentially stressful endeavour! I have set down basic guidelines to follow, and pointed out many of the pitfalls which could take an unprepared tutor by surprise.

A professional instructor learns their craft through experience and practise. It is not just a case of telling someone what to do... that would be easy. We must know what to say and when to say it, when to speak and when to be quiet. We must always be ready in case instructions are carried out wrongly or not carried out at all. Knowing where errors are most commonly made can go a long way towards averting possible disaster. The purpose of this book is to give you the benefit of someone else's experience, so that you can hopefully, avoid making many of the mistakes that an instructor will make during the first years of their 'apprenticeship'.

Firstly though, you must prepare yourself. The law requires you to be over 21, with at least three years' qualified driving behind you. Do you feel experienced and knowledgeable enough to take on the responsibility of teaching someone to drive? When was the last time you looked at a copy of the Highway Code? Too many drivers let basic standards slip after passing the L test and lapse into 'bad habits'. These habits are not just bad but often potentially dangerous and it is essential that they are not passed on to the learner.

Rules and regulations are constantly changing. You may not know as much as you think you do about modern driving so this is a good time to start brushing up. Get hold of a copy of the Highway Code and do some studying.

Better still; buy a copy of the Driver & Vehicle Standards Agency (DVSA) manual *'Driving'*, available from most booksellers. This book is sometimes called the 'driving instructors bible' and it's a worthwhile investment.

I recommend Driving because I am not going to waste time in trying to teach you to drive. This you can do already, but you will find the manual an invaluable reference to fill in whatever gaps your knowledge may have, particularly with regard to the DVSA standard of motoring. What I am aiming to do is to show you how to pass on this knowledge to others.

Of course your pupil must have a valid provisional licence before taking to the road, but you must also make sure that their eyesight is up to an acceptable standard.

For the purpose of the driving test, a candidate must be able to read a vehicle number plate from a minimum distance of 20 metres. This as far as I am concerned is a totally inadequate standard for safe driving. Make sure to check your pupil's eyesight from a greater distance. Nerves can affect eyesight on the day of the test and we certainly wouldn't want the test abandoned due to poor vision. Better still, a visit to an optician may not be a bad idea, and why not take this opportunity to do the same yourself? It can be surprising how much your eyesight deteriorates over a period of years without you even noticing.

DRIVING SCHOOLS

There may come a point when you want your pupil to take some extra training or an assessment with a professional instructor. I would not recommend that you do this too soon, as the instructor's method of training may differ from what you are doing and this would confuse the trainee. But once they have gone beyond the novice stages and are showing signs of independence, then that may be the time to seek the opinion of another person to help put the final 'polish' on your work... but if you decide to do this then you should choose with care.

Approved Driving Instructors (ADIs), need to pass qualifying exams and be registered with the DVSA in order to charge for lessons. An ADI must display a pink (part qualified) or green (fully qualified) certificate on the windscreen of their car when they are doing this.

Unfortunately, because of serious flaws in the DVSA testing process, a lot of people can easily qualify for the ADI register even though they are not very good at what they do. There are a lot of very poor quality ADIs, and once an instructor does get onto the register, even though they may be notoriously bad at what they do, the DVSA is either unwilling or powerless to do anything about it. An ADI may repeatedly bring a very poor standard for test, including dangerous candidates, but the DVSA rarely takes any serious action to remedy this.

The DVSA does operate a system of 'standards checks' on ADIs; once every few years an examiner will sit in the back of a lesson to assess the instructors ability and award them a grade, but these 'lessons' can easily be rehearsed in advance and are all too easy to get around by those who know how to play the game.

Find out what grade your potential instructor is. On the older system which is now being updated, 6 is the highest, and I would not choose anyone with less than a grade 5. Grade 4 is too easy to obtain and anything below this is substandard. ADIs graded under the newer system will either get A, B or fail. To be on the safe side I would insist on someone with only the highest grade!

You may see advertising where instructors are claiming to have proof of high pass rates, this may be true, but then again this is something which can easily be manipulated. An ADI's personal number will be taken from their certificate when they bring someone for test, and the data from these tests is then compiled to produce statistics. A rogue instructor will simply remove their badge when they're expecting a test failure and leave it in when they're expecting a pass, in order to make it look as though they have a higher percentage of passes than they actually do.

Another point to be aware of, especially with larger driving schools, is the variation in ability from one instructor to the next. A tutor employed by a school, is not necessarily one trained by that same establishment. Most driving schools operate on a franchise basis and are willing to take on any instructor, regardless of ability. The new recruit, in return for paying a franchise fee, is then given a car with a famous name written all over it and sets off to work. The instructor's method of tuition is rarely checked before agreeing to the franchise so, as a result, you may go to what you believe is the best driving school in the country and end up with the worst instructor in town. This does happen... I've worked with a few!

When choosing your driving school don't try to make any false economies. People often complain about the cost of driving lessons; but when you compare the cost of a one-hour session to the amount a plumber or mechanic would charge for an hour's work, driving lessons are not that expensive! You should avoid cheap lessons and 'special offers', a good instructor should not need to sell themselves cheaply.

A personal recommendation may sound great, but novice drivers generally have no idea what a good instructor is, or whether they are being taught correctly. Too often people recommend their instructors because they are 'nice', or they have a laugh with them. You need more than this in order to make an informed choice! It is very difficult and I wish I could be more positive about this, but the only way I would trust a recommendation, is from pupils (and preferably several) who have already passed with an ADI, and the vast majority of those people should be passing at first or second attempt in order to be trusted as evidence of good training.

YOU, THE INSTRUCTOR

Now, on to you as the instructor; are you prepared for what to expect? Too many friends and relatives who try teaching each other wind up arguing in the car, often because of a lack of patience and understanding from the qualified driver.

Patience is the keyword. Just because changing gear is second nature to you, don't expect a beginner to have the same ability. Things like co-ordinating the movements incorporated in a change of gear and deciding when a change is necessary can take time to develop. Think about how much practise you have had since your first lesson -practise can make complicated operations seem very simple.

Some experienced motorists fail to understand why learners have problems with apparently easy tasks such as moving off without stalling. This shows a lack of memory on their part. Try to recall the difficulties you had as a learner driver.

Remember how many times you stalled the car at traffic lights, the occasions you pulled out in front of another vehicle at the wrong moment and the times you were afraid to move at all. And the instructions you were given which you failed to hear or simply misunderstood and went on to do something entirely different, the number of attempts it took before getting that reversing right... we all went through it didn't we? The problem is that people forget how hard it really was and it all seems so simple after years of practise.

Have patience. If your pupil doesn't get it right first time, let them try again. Give a second or third explanation if necessary and if this fails to work try putting it in a different manner. Demonstrate, if need be, by taking over the driving seat and showing what should be done. But above all you must be patient!

You may be lucky enough to have a pupil with natural co-ordination, and someone who has watched while you are driving and managed to learn from the experience. But if your learner seems to be disoriented and lacking in any basic road sense, you must refrain from snapping or shouting. This will only make them feel worse and increase the problems. Mistakes are often a result of nothing more than nerves... you must keep control over yourself and try to encourage the driver to keep trying when things are going wrong. If you can remain calm and relaxed this will start to rub off on the beginner, thus making it easier for them to settle down which, in return, will make your job simpler.

So, now you have committed yourself and promised to be a calm and patient tutor, you have decided (hopefully) to do some studying of your own in addition to reading this book.

Now what else needs to be done?

THE TRAINING VEHICLE

We will assume your vehicle is taxed and covered by an MOT certificate (where applicable), but has it been insured for the learner driver and is it roadworthy? Although these things should be a matter of routine, make sure that everything is sound and legal with the training vehicle, particularly if this is the one you intend to eventually use for the driving test.

There are some vehicles which may have had safety recalls by the manufacturer, and not all of these are widely advertised. On the DVSA website you will find information about those cars which may not be suitable for a driving test unless they satisfy certain conditions, check to make sure yours is not one of these.

Insurance can be very expensive for beginners, but if you do an internet search you will find companies who specialise in short term insurance for leaner drivers. Using these you can get temporary cover for a few months at a time without breaking the bank.

The vehicle will of course, need to be equipped with L plates. These must be clearly visible to the front and rear of the car, but not stuck in the windscreen! This can be a dangerous obstruction to vision, as can anything dangling from rear-view mirrors. Hanging decorations are also very distracting and if you do have any I strongly recommend that they are removed.

L plates come in several varieties; adhesive, tie on, fully magnetic and those with a magnetic strip on the top and bottom edges. When driving the car yourself, L plates should be removed, so, for this reason, and because they can damage the paintwork, adhesive plates are not to be recommended. Most people tend to leave the plates on indefinitely once they have been attached to a car; but they are meant to be a warning to other road users that the vehicle is in the hands of an inexperienced driver who is likely to make mistakes. They should be removed when a qualified driver is behind the wheel otherwise there is little point having the things in use. Tie on or magnetic plates are better.

Of the two types of magnetic L, the fully magnetic ones give an all-over grip but can be difficult to put in place on curved surfaces. If an edge or corner is left even slightly raised they can soon be lifted off by the wind. The plates with magnetic strips can also suffer from wind problems, but being more flexible can be affixed to practically any surface. These are probably your best bet but it will depend on the design of your car.

It is essential to furnish yourself with at least one extra rear-view mirror. Detachable ones are available from most motoring accessory shops for a few pounds. It is very important to be constantly aware of what is happening behind and alongside while guiding a learner through traffic. The safety of the vehicle is your responsibility. The extra mirror should be fixed to the screen just to the left of the normal mirror and will afford a reasonable view directly behind and to the right (offside), but the left side (nearside) will be hidden from view. For this reason you may find it useful to attach a second, smaller mirror in the top left-hand corner of the screen.

The second mirror will serve a dual purpose. Firstly, it covers the blind spot on your left, revealing any cycles or mopeds that may creep up otherwise unseen. Secondly, it can be swivelled to the right to show the driver's eyes in action. Some people make very little head movement when using mirrors or looking from side to side. If you have any problems detecting proper mirror work from your pupil, the second mirror will make the job simple.

Now we are all set to go. Your job may be relatively easy or very difficult and, who knows, you may even give up half-way through! I will make no impossible claims like guaranteeing a first-time pass, or that using this book will make teaching someone to drive simple - it's just not that easy. Even the best instructors experience problems with difficult pupils.

I cannot work miracles for you; all I can do is pass on the benefit of my experience as a professional instructor in the hope that you can use the advice to craft your novice into a competent driver who will obtain that elusive first-time pass. I have earned a first-time pass rate second to none, but have never been so silly as to guarantee against failure. Even the best trained drivers can suffer from nerves on the day. If you sit in the back of the car on test you may see something entirely different from the pupil you taught - at that point it is out of your hands.

The only claim I am prepared to make is that the teaching method set out in this book has been proven to be successful, and if the principles are adhered to and the learner is given enough practise, there is no reason that the pupil shouldn't pass at the first attempt. But that depends on four things:

- How well you can put the ideas across

- How readily the pupil can absorb the teaching
- Whether they are co-ordinated or can learn to co-ordinate through practise
- Whether they have enough experience and practise to cope with the nerves and pressure of a driving test situation.

The following text will show you how to go about teaching the way a professional does. It explains how to prevent mistakes and overcome problems, points out what kind of things may go wrong and the difficulties you are likely to encounter. Your learner will almost certainly give you a few problems, but perhaps the most troublesome aspect of teaching someone to drive is dealing with other road users. Thankfully, we do come across a section of the public who have time for a smile as the learner passes by or moves on after a couple of stalls, but there seems to be an increasing number of drivers, cyclists and pedestrians whose ignorance, impatience and downright stupidity can conjure up situations much more dangerous than the pupils themselves could have gotten into.

Throughout all this, you as the instructor, must remain unflappable and tolerant and under pressure be capable of talking a new driver through every movement as if your words were strings connected to the pupil's limbs. They must be guided through each single operation until the time comes when they can start to think for themselves. The one big problem here is that whatever you instruct the novice to do, there is no guarantee that they will do it. This is where your experience as a driver and your reactions come in. So even if you are lucky enough to be training someone who seems to be a natural driving talent, never take your eyes off the road for more than an instant.

If those last chilling words have not frightened you off, I cannot say much for your sanity except that it will help you through these coming months! Now for a short summary:

- Study the Highway Code and Driving
- Make sure the pupil is insured to drive your vehicle; that they have a valid licence, and their eyesight is at least up to the legally required standard
- Fix the L plates in a clearly visible position, not in the windows
- Obtain yourself at least one detachable rear-view mirror
- Ensure constant and regular practise for the learner
- Be patient, do not expect a beginner to be able to do everything first time
- If you use a driving school at any stage, avoid cheap offers and make certain the instructor has a high grade and a good proven pass rate
- And finally, remember that you were a learner once!

2
THE FIRST LESSON

A beginner's first lesson will understandably have them feeling a little nervous and perhaps you too, will feel some apprehension if you are exploring unknown territory. You are the pupil's confidence to begin with so you must at least appear to be relaxed, even if you don't really feel that way.

Many new drivers are afraid of the car they are going to drive; they may not understand how it works and wonder what is going to happen. It will help if they are first introduced to the machine by going over a few simple routine tasks of maintenance. These are things that should be done on a regular basis anyway and ought to be an integral part of a driver's education. We will assume at this point that our learner knows nothing about the car engine.

Show them under the bonnet and explain what the routine checks are, how to read the oil level, where oil goes, and do the same for coolant level, washer bottles etc., topping up as necessary. Then get them to check over the tyres with you and show how to adjust the pressures. Finally, point out where the fuel goes and don't forget at some stage to take the novice to a petrol station and explain how to fill the tank. These are things a professional instructor rarely has time to go through with a pupil, and one area where you have a distinct advantage; you do not have to work to any deadlines. Make the most of your advantage and be thorough with the training.

In-car training can begin at several stages. If you are helping a friend or relative who has had plenty of experience and recent practise, perhaps they may be allowed to sit straight in the driving seat. If they haven't driven your type of car before, show them the controls and how they operate before attempting to drive off. Make sure the pupil has gone through the normal procedure of checking that doors are closed, adjusting seat and mirrors and, of course, putting on the seatbelt, some will forget the basics.

Once on the move it is advisable to keep to fairly quiet areas initially. This gives the driver time to settle down and become accustomed to the car. It also gives you the chance to assess their level of skill before deciding to venture out into any sort of traffic.

With a new driver, or relatively inexperienced person, however, a different approach is needed. Firstly, tell them that you are going to drive to a quiet area where you will be able to explain the controls of the car. For a complete beginner, a quiet park or clear stretch of road is the best venue, otherwise choose a quiet estate where you will not meet much traffic. You will have to drive the pupil away and bring them back after the lesson for the first few sessions. Exactly how many will depend on how quickly the novice progresses and how busy the area is.

Upon reaching the chosen place, stop in a quiet spot and invite the pupil into the driving seat. You must make certain that they look round before opening the car door, whether they are getting into or out of the vehicle. Many people forget this very important safety check, and will swing doors open regardless of how it affects others. You are the pupil's eyes and ears at this stage, always be one step ahead of them.

Having gained your seats, the driver with some previous experience; after being introduced to the car's controls if necessary, can then show you what they are capable of; ask them to carry out a few simple exercises at first such as moving off and stopping, turning left and right, and pulling out from behind parked cars (angle starts). Step in where necessary to help the driver along and correct any mistakes, though be careful not to jump on every minor fault straight away as this could upset the pupil's confidence. Next, move on to the manoeuvres: the emergency stop, reversing, turning in the road - (three point turn) - and also the reverse parking exercises.

It may be that on previous lessons the learner has only covered approaching junctions and is not yet at the stage where they are ready to tackle manoeuvres. If this is the case, work on what they already know and improve where possible before going on to teach something new. You will find out how to teach the manoeuvres in a later chapter.

Complete beginners must first be given a full explanation of the cockpit drill on entering a vehicle, followed by a detailed lesson on the car controls. This will help new drivers understand a little of how the machine behaves, and when they are being instructed to employ a particular control they should realise why it is being used and what effect it ought to have.

THE COCKPIT DRILL

The cockpit drill should begin with the simple check of ensuring that the doors are properly closed, they do not always catch first time. In the event of having to re-close the door, teach your pupil that a check over the right-hand shoulder must be taken before it is opened to ensure that no danger is caused to any passing people or vehicles. The door can then be re-closed a bit more firmly.

We now need to get the driver into a comfortable seating position. The most important thing about adjustment of the driving seat is that the pupil can reach all the controls without difficulty. It should be positioned so that the driver is able to depress the clutch fully without stretching or being cramped; the leg should appear relaxed and slightly bent at the knee. While talking a novice through the adjustment of the seat, refer to the left-hand pedal rather than the clutch as they may not yet know what a clutch is.

To check the rake angle of the seat, have your student place both hands on the steering wheel at the 12 o'clock point - arms should be slightly bent and shoulders comfortably resting on the seat back. Even if the seat is set up correctly, show how it may be moved for future reference. If your car has such things as an adjustable steering wheel etc, then of course you should also cover these.

An important point to remember is that the head restraint is correctly adjusted so that the back of the head is properly supported. Rear end shunts from following vehicles are one of the commonest types of accident, and learner drivers who may be slow to move away or stall at junctions are particularly at risk from this. A properly adjusted restraint can help prevent whiplash injuries; make sure the passenger seat is also set up correctly for you.

Some people may still have a problem reaching the controls if they are particularly small. To compensate for this, use a cushion or two to boost the driver upwards or forwards if necessary.

Finally the seatbelts, it is unlikely that your pupil will not know how to fasten one but make sure they are both worn!

Mirrors come next, one of the most important aids to safe driving. I cannot over-emphasise how important it is to teach the proper use of mirrors, and here the driving manual is invaluable with advice on the subject. Ensure the pupil knows how to adjust the interior mirror for the fullest view through the rear window, and that both door mirrors are set up so they can see clearly what may be alongside the vehicle on both sides. I do need to stress here that contrary to what some drivers believe; the nearside door mirror is NOT the 'reversing mirror'!

As a frequent cyclist I have lost count of the number of drivers who pull to the left causing me to brake as I shout a warning, before they then present the excuse 'Sorry I didn't see you!' What they mean as that they don't know what the nearside mirror is for.

Once the mirrors are properly adjusted, emphasise the importance of using them regularly while driving. Also explain the significance of blind spots, not just in the mirrors but any other blind areas your car has. Include a warning about the door pillars on either side of the front windscreen, behind which approaching two-wheelers may be hidden from view. They also restrict your view when driving through bends. Ensure the pupil is made aware of this danger and instruct them to move their head when necessary to get a proper view past the door pillars and so eliminate the possibility of something being missed.

While on the subject of rear observation, point out the need for an over the shoulder look before moving off from the kerbside. This is something we are all taught during driving lessons, but how many become lazy and start to rely on the mirrors alone?

Get the pupil to look into the right-hand door mirror and ask them to describe what they can see, and what is the nearest thing to the car they can pick out? There will almost certainly be something out of view that they miss such as a lamppost, tree, or even a driveway; then ask them to imagine what would happen if they were to drive off just as someone was coming onto the road alongside them from that hidden bind spot.

Next thing on the agenda is to teach the new driver about the controls of the car, where they are and how they operate.

THE CONTROLS LESSON

Giving a complete novice a full and detailed explanation of the controls of a car can take some time. It would, therefore, be sensible to make the first lesson of one and a half to two hours duration. This allows time for theoretical tuition and leaves time for practise as well.

There is no point going into great detail when covering every control, some things are more important than others at this stage. Minor controls need not be fully explained as long as their location is pointed out. The following is how I would give a controls lesson.

Inform the pupil that you are going to talk about each control in turn beginning with the foot controls. Point to these in order to get the student to look at what you are commenting on. Then begin:

"As you can see, there are three pedals to be controlled by the feet. They are from right to left, A, B, and C - accelerator, brake and clutch. We will start with the accelerator."

Accelerator

"The accelerator is controlled by your right foot; it's a very light and sensitive pedal which should always be used smoothly and evenly. Very little pressure is needed to move it, if you carefully press it down just a little you will see."

"The function of the accelerator is to control the amount of power going to the engine. When the engine is running, there is a mixture of air and fuel being fed to it, which is ignited by a spark to create a small explosion. From this little explosion comes a gas which drives a cylinder to power the engine. That's

why I'm going to refer to it as the gas pedal from now on. The further down the gas pedal is pressed the more power the engine has, and vice versa. As you take your foot off the pedal the power is reduced."

"A little later on, when we are getting ready to move off I'll ask you to 'set' the gas. What I mean by that is to lightly press the pedal so we get a lively, steady hum from the engine."

Footbrake

"Now we move on to the footbrake, the middle of the three pedals. Like the gas pedal it's operated by the right foot. When the brake is pressed, red lights show at the back of the car to warn other people that we're slowing down or stopping."

"The harder the pedal is pressed, the faster the car will lose speed, but the pressure you use should always be smooth and progressive, light at first and then gradually increasing. The footbrake has a spongy feel - press it a few times. When taking your foot from the gas pedal to use the brake, you need not lift up your whole foot. The best way is to place your heel between both pedals and use that as a pivot."

(Demonstrate this movement with your hand).

"Don't actually press the pedals, but just practise moving your right foot from the brake to the gas pedal and back while keeping your heel on the floor."

(People with smaller feet may not actually be able to do this and will have to move their whole foot.)

"At some stage while we are driving I'll ask you to 'cover' the brake. This means that you should put your right foot over the pedal without actually touching it; then you'll be ready to use it as soon as I give the instruction."

Clutch

"The left-hand pedal, the clutch, is quite different from the other two. This is operated by the left foot, and unlike the gas and brake pedals it doesn't matter how quickly it is pressed down. But what is really important is how the pedal comes back up. It works on a spring principle, so if it is let up too sharply it would bounce, causing the car to jerk. Therefore it must always be brought up smoothly. If you move the pedal up and down you will feel the spring in action."

"The clutch is basically a means of connecting and disconnecting the engine from the wheels of the car."

(Show the pupil Fig.1)

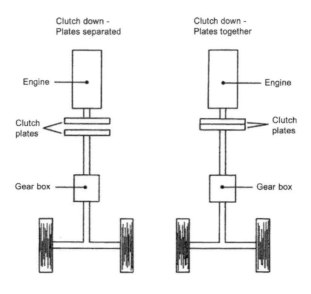

Figure 1. How the clutch operates

"Without going into too much detail, the clutch consists of two plates, one is connected to the engine and turns all the time it is running. The second plate is linked to the wheels. When the clutch pedal is fully up there is the spring I mentioned which holds the two plates together. When it is pushed down the plates are separated and the link between engine and wheels is broken. But there is an intermediate stage."

"When preparing the car for moving off, the clutch pedal is brought up until the two plates just begin to touch. This is called

the biting point. When this point is reached you will hear a change in the sound of the engine, it will become lower. You might also feel a slight pull forward which happens when the link is completed between the engine and the wheels. We will practise finding the biting point later on."

"As with the brake, at some stage I'll ask you to cover the clutch, in this case it's your left foot, of course, over the pedal without making contact."

"I'll go through the main hand controls with you now, starting with the steering wheel."

Steering Wheel

"When you're not turning the steering wheel, keep your hands between the positions corresponding to ten-to-two, and a quarter-to-three on a clock face. Try to keep your hands relaxed as there is no need to grip the wheel tightly. When you need to steer, don't cross your hands, use a push and pull movement. When you want to turn to the left, for Instance, pull the wheel down with your left hand, and slide your right hand down the opposite side."

(Demonstrate the movement)

"Then push the wheel up with the right hand, and slide the left hand upward. Using this method rather than crossing your hands gives a better balance and a safer control over the steering. When you want to straighten up, use the same

technique but in the opposite direction. After a turn, the steering will feel like it wants to straighten itself up, but you mustn't be tempted to let the wheel spin back through your hands. If the wheels hit a bump or pothole while doing this the steering could easily be thrown off course."

Handbrake (Parking Brake)

As the location and type of parking brake may differ from one vehicle to the next, you may have to change the narrative to suit. The following description is based on the most common type of ratchet parking brake, but first of all you may have to indicate where it is.

"On to the parking brake now; it isn't used for stopping the car, but should be applied once the vehicle has halted to make sure it remains stationary, especially when there is a slope. In most cases, it operates on just the two rear wheels of the car and when applied it helps to prevent the wheels from moving."

"The parking brake is applied at the moment, before we practise using it I want you to press your right foot on the footbrake to make sure the car doesn't move when the parking brake is released. Keep your foot on the brake for the moment. To release the brake, you must first lift it a little higher than it is now, then press the button on the end so it can be lowered."

"To re-apply it, the button must be pressed in first, then lift it until you feel some resistance and let go of the button. If you fail to press the button properly when applying the parking

brake you will hear a grating noise. That is the ratchet which holds the brake in place. Applying the brake without releasing the ratchet just causes unnecessary wear."

When the pupil has been allowed to operate the parking brake a few times, ensure it is in the applied position and tell them to remove their foot from the footbrake as the car is now secure again.

The Gear Lever

For the purpose of this narrative, we will assume that we are dealing with a standard five speed gearbox, though if you have more or less gears, teach the use of them all. Most cars will happily cruise around town in fifth gear, yet many people still think that fifth gear is only for motorways! Ensure you are in neutral before starting.

"The third main hand control is the gear lever."

(Touch it to bring their attention to it)

"It is used to change the engine from one gear to another. Where the lever lies now is the neutral position, the car is not in gear and the lever can be moved easily from side to side."

(Get the learner to try this)

"Whenever the car is stationary for a length of time, neutral should be selected."

"This car has five gears for forward driving and one for reversing, for the time being though we're just going to use the first four. To move the lever you must first put the clutch pedal down and you can then move the lever to the position you want to select. First gear is the most powerful and is the one we normally use to move the car from rest. Each gear works best within a certain speed range, you will find out more about this when we come to changing gears later."

"When moving the gear lever, always use the palm of your hand rather than grasping it. For first and second gear your palm should be facing towards me."

(Refer to Fig. 2 and show this diagram to the pupil)

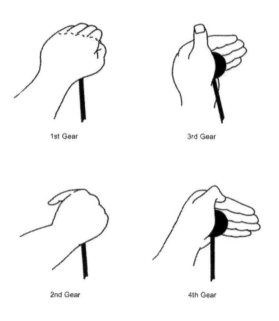

Figure 2. Movement of the gear lever

"For third and fourth gear, turn the palm towards yourself. This makes moving the lever easier and helps prevent you from getting into the wrong gear. I want you to practise moving the gear lever from one position to another while the engine is switched off. Put the clutch down, and hold it down for now, face your palm towards me on the lever as the diagram shows and select first gear."

You must now talk the pupil through each movement of the gear lever from first up to fourth, and back down through the positions. Try this a few times, the student will no doubt be looking down at the control while they are doing this, so tell them to look through the front screen at some object outside the car and go through all the positions several times more. Ensure that they understand the rule about not looking down when changing gear, eyes must be kept on the road.

After this exercise, instruct the learner to select neutral and to relax the foot from the clutch. Ask if there are any questions on the main controls and clear these up if necessary, then carry on the tuition with the minor controls. You may have to alter a few details to suit the vehicle you are using.

Indicators

"I'll go through the minor controls now, starting with the indicators. These are a way of warning other people of what you intend to do next. The lever that operates the indicators is on the left of the steering column, here. The lever is moved up to

signal right, and down for left. When the indicators are in use, there is a flashing green light on the dashboard and you will hear a ticking sound."

(Show where the light is located)

"When you have signalled and finished the move, the signal must be cancelled and that can be done in two different ways. There is a self-cancelling device which is worked by the steering. After indicating and moving to the right, for Instance, when the steering wheel is brought back to the left the signal will automatically cancel. When the steering movement has only been slight this may not work, so you must carry out the other option which is to cancel it yourself. Don't try to cancel the signal though while you are doing any steering, wait until you've finished turning."

The Horn

Many people seem to be unaware of what the horn is really for, mainly I think, because few learners are taught when to use it. Start your student off on the right note!

"In the centre of the steering wheel is the horn. It's not there to attract the attention of your friends, or to avoid the need to get out of the car and knock on someone's door when you call to pick them up! It's a means of warning other people that you are around. For instance, if you're driving along and you notice the front of a car creeping out of a junction ahead and you're not sure that the driver can see you, let them hear

you. A tap on the horn will let them know you are there. Or if you spot children playing behind parked cars or in the road, don't take chances with them. If they are intent on their games they may not notice you - a tap on the horn will make sure they know you are coming. Don't be frightened to use it as sounding the horn at the right time can help prevent accidents.

Other Controls

These include wipers and washers, lights, demisters etc. All these minor controls do not require a detailed explanation at this early stage, unless it is actually raining or dark during the first lesson, but you should briefly show where they are.

On future lessons the other controls should be introduced and operated on a regular basis. Part of the driving test includes two 'safety questions' one in the car park and one on the move, where the candidate will be required to either explain, or demonstrate the use of various controls. They must also know how to check the tyres, fluid levels etc. A current list of these questions is available from the DVSA website. You should get hold of a copy of this and go through them regularly with your pupil.

The controls lesson shouldn't be rushed. The principles that appear simple to you may take some time for a novice who has never before sat in the driving seat to understand. Once all the facts have been explained ask your student a few questions to see if they really have understood, and don't be worried or irritable if anything has to be repeated. It is much better if the beginner has no uncertainty.

At the end of this part of the lesson the pupil is ready to start the engine.

STARTING THE ENGINE

Firstly, teach the driver how to take proper precautions before starting the engine, by checking that the parking brake is firmly applied and then that the gear lever is in neutral.

When this routine has been covered, hand the pupil the ignition key - this should never be left in place when you leave the driving seat. If a novice is ready to go with the key in place and you are still walking around the car to get into the other side, how can you claim to be fully in charge of the situation? Also, if a learner is accustomed to the key being in place already when entering the car, they could be in trouble the first time they have to put it in if they don't know how to tackle a steering lock. If this first time is when taking the driving test it won't do much to help settle the nerves!

Starting routines do differ from car to car, especially with modern 'keyless' ignitions and various other developments. You may need to adapt instructions to suit, but here we will deal with a standard key ignition. Hand the key over, explain where it goes, and tell the pupil to put it in but without turning it.

"When the key is turned it goes through three positions. The first releases the steering lock, that's just a security device. If you carefully turn the key away from yourself a little you should hear a click as the lock releases. If you ever find that the key won't turn just move the steering wheel up or down a little, that will enable the key to move. In the first position you can also operate some of the minor controls. The second position is the ignition. Carefully turn the key away from yourself again until the lights show on the dashboard. You should always check that those lights are working before starting the engine."

(Ensure the pupil knows what these warning lights mean.)

"If you stall the car at any time those same lights will come on to let you know that the engine has stopped. With the switch in the ignition position all the main electrical controls can be operated. The third and last position is the starter itself. We're not going to start the engine just yet, I'll tell you what we need to do first. So for the time being, turn the key back towards yourself to switch off the Ignition."

"To start the engine, the first thing you have to do is to hold the clutch down with your left foot. Then the key can be turned to the ignition position. To get the engine running the key must be turned fully away from yourself. When you do that you will hear the engine turning. Sometimes it will start straight away, other times they key will have to be held for several seconds, but as soon as you hear the engine start I want you to release the key, you can then ease your foot away from the clutch pedal. Okay... ready to switch on?"

You must now talk the pupil through the starting procedure while they carry out the actions.

With the engine running, the first skill to be taught is finding the biting point. When teaching even this basic exercise there is a rule to be followed; each time you require the pupil to use a control tell them how it should be used before mentioning the pedal itself. Descriptive words such as smoothly and slowly are important to a novice driver. This way 'lightly' press on the gas pedal should be easily understood, whereas 'press' the gas pedal down, to a heavy footed learner could have unfortunate consequences! Always be careful to think how you put instructions across and never take anything for granted.

FINDING THE BITING POINT

Instruct your pupil along these lines:

"We're going to practise finding the biting point now, if you remember that's when the two clutch plates first begin to touch. First thing is to put the clutch down and keep it down for the moment, then face your palm towards me on the lever and select first gear position. Now very lightly press on the accelerator to set the gas so we get a steady hum, that's it, keep your right foot still. Now listen to the engine and slowly bring the clutch up until you hear the sound of the engine change then keep your foot steady. There... did you hear it? That's the biting point. Put the clutch down now and take your foot off the gas,

move the gear lever into neutral, and relax your feet. We'll try that again now."

Even this simplest of driving skills may not go right first time. Often the vehicle will stall or begin moving off because the novice brings the clutch up too high. In the event of a stall, instruct the pupil to check that the parking brake is on and to select neutral before restarting the engine. Sometimes the gear lever will stick after stalling and the clutch must be depressed before it will go into neutral. You will have to tell the driver to do this if they have taken their foot from the pedal, which many tend to do when they realise something is going wrong.

Stalling can be a regular occurrence with learner drivers and the number of stalls can vary greatly from person to person depending on how well they are co-ordinated. These stalls are usually a source of irritation to other drivers, but you must teach your novice not to worry if the car stalls, nor to rush the restarting procedure, even if you are out in traffic at a later stage and some impatient driver sounds the horn. Tell your pupil to take their time. Rushing only makes things worse and will result in more stalling. Each time a stall occurs in the early stages, the driver must carry out the parking brake and neutral routine despite the bit of extra time this takes. As an experienced driver, you might be in the habit of simply holding the clutch down while you do a 'rolling restart' after a stall, but you cannot rely on a novice to do this. They will absent-mindedly take their foot from the pedal, and if the starter is then turned with the engine in gear, a sudden forward movement could be dangerous. They will also panic if the car starts to roll back.

If the car begins moving forward while attempting to find the biting point, give the instruction:

"Clutch down, off gas."

Brief and straight to the point; this works best for emergency situations as you may not have time to fit in full sentences. Most people should be able to find the biting point without much difficulty, but if control begins to slip away, a good firm tug on the parking brake will halt the car's progress so make sure yours is well adjusted!

Once you have found the biting point successfully, practise this several times and then have the pupil switch off. They are now ready to drive but must be made aware of two things before attempting to move off... 'normal driving position' and 'adequate clearance'.

Direct them to try to keep the vehicle about three feet from the kerb or verge while on the move. Some practise will be needed before they can judge this accurately. If a tendency is shown for drifting when you begin driving, assist the pupil with the steering by gently guiding them onto the correct course and then telling them to try and maintain the line, but do not keep hold of the wheel for longer than is really necessary.

Adequate clearance has to be mentioned because you are almost certain to encounter one or two parked cars along the way. When passing stationary obstructions, tell your pupil that they need to be given clearance of at least the width of an open door wherever possible; when this is not possible then a low speed should be maintained while the cars are passed.

MOVING OFF AND STOPPING

We can now turn our attention to the business of moving off and stopping. You should explain that finding the biting point is the first part of this procedure - the preparation. Then tell your pupil that in a moment you will teach them how to move away, and once on the move you will drive for a short distance before you pick a suitable stopping place. You will talk them through the method for stopping the car when the time comes. Now talk them through starting the engine again and finding the biting point then continue:

"Now that we're ready to move off we must make sure it's safe, so check the mirrors, and keeping your feet still, look over your right-hand shoulder to see if anything is hidden in the blind spot."

(Look round yourself)

"It's clear at the moment so now you can release the parking brake."

At this point the car may or may not begin moving. If it does, instruct:

"Keep your feet still."

If not, add one more instruction before this:

"Slowly bring the clutch up till the car moves then keep your feet still."

Then from either of these two beginnings carry on with:

"Steer to the normal driving position; slowly bring the clutch up fully and check the mirrors once more."

Hopefully you should now be moving along at a nice slow speed, the novice now needs a little time to get the feel of being on the move.

Having fully engaged the clutch, do make certain the pupil takes away the foot properly, riding or slipping of the clutch must be discouraged from the outset to prevent it developing into a habit. Many drivers who do this have a tendency to put the clutch down without even realising they are doing it. This happens in particular when approaching turns and unless the clutch is fully engaged the car is not properly under control. Make sure your driver understands that the clutch pedal is an important control, not a foot rest!

The length of time you should allow the pupil to drive before finding a stopping place depends on how they are controlling the car so far. Someone who moved off smoothly and can manage to steer a reasonably straight line will only need a short distance between moving away and stopping. A less able driver needs to be allowed a little more time to settle. Either way it won't be too long before you need to direct the pupil to a parking position.

Choice of words and timing of instructions are important factors when teaching someone to drive. If you want to stop in a specific place, ensure the driver understands this before you start the instructions for slowing down.

When you want to halt, forewarn the pupil:

"As we pass the next car I'm going to talk you through the procedure for stopping. We are aiming to stop when we are about level with the second tree."

This is clear and unmistakable whereas:

"I want you to stop after the next car," might well have the driver going for the brake before you have chance to mention the next car. As soon as they hear the word stop they are thinking 'how?' and might not even hear the last remark let alone wait for the instructions. Tread carefully, especially if your pupil is of a nervous disposition.

Instruction for stopping is delivered along these lines:

"Check mirrors, indicate down for left (if necessary), ease off the gas and cover the brake. Gently steer to the left into a parking position and cover the clutch."

You may need to assist the steering in order to bring the car to a reasonable distance from the kerb, but don't try to get a new driver to come in too close, you don't want the tyres kerbing!

Final instructions are:

"Straighten the steering wheel, check mirrors, gently brake and clutch down, keep your feet still. Apply the parking brake, select neutral."

The command 'keep your feet still' will crop up quite often in the instructions. Absent minded beginners will take their feet from the controls at the wrong time if you don't give constant reminders. This normally happens after stopping when they want to sit back and relax after the ordeal of a 50 metre drive.

You will probably need to give a beginner total instruction throughout the early stages, talking them through every move they make. This will be necessary until the pupil begins to get used to routines and starts performing them without your prompting. Each new topic introduced will also require full instruction initially; few people can take to driving immediately and most need constant reminding of apparently simple things like putting the clutch down before stopping. You must never assume that once your pupil has been told to do something that they will do it next time automatically. Some will need a lot of help.

This is where many people who attempt driving instruction go wrong. When you drive yourself many basic operations are carried out without the need for conscious thought. You may find it hard to understand why the novice in the driving neat needs to be told the same thing time and again. That's why patience and understanding is so important. You may also find it difficult to talk the learner through routines which suddenly seem complicated when all the individual actions are broken down, but you can practise this when driving yourself.

Try an advanced driving technique called the 'running commentary'. What it entails is for you to think aloud, describe what you can see on the road ahead, behind and to the sides, say what you think is likely to happen next and what you are going to do about it. Talk yourself through each movement you make, when you move off, change gear, turn corners, check mirrors and change lanes. Think about each action you have to carry out for these manoeuvres. If you can do this it will give you some idea of what you will need to be saying to your pupil, and with practise the words will flow more easily.

Practising Moving off and Stopping

Moving off and stopping needs to be practised until the learner is able to do both reasonably smoothly, and can bring the car to a halt in the exact place which you picked out. We are not looking for a beginner to reach a level of near perfection, so long as there is no excessive jerkiness or repeated stalling. There will be ample time to improve later on, as there will be plenty more stops and starts during the next stage which is the teaching of gear changing.

Angle Starts and Hill Starts

When starting a new driver off from scratch, moving off at a sharp angle or on a hill should be avoided until the learner has developed a certain amount of control over the vehicle. Staying completely clear of these exercises can be difficult at times though... where do we find a road devoid of parked cars these days?

Teaching a pupil the normal procedure for moving off should prepare them for any slight gradients that may be met on the first lesson or two, so there will be no need to explain hill starts just yet, but the same cannot always be said for angle starts (moving out from behind a parked car).

At some stage during the first drive, you may find yourself stopping a little or a lot further forward than you had anticipated. As a result, an obstruction may prevent you from moving away normally. This is the moment, of course, when an angle start must be introduced.

To accustom an inexperienced person to pulling out from behind a parked car, plenty of space must be left initially between your vehicle and the obstruction. What seems like plenty of room to you will appear to be a lot less to a new driver. It can take them quite a while in learning to judge the size of the vehicle in relation to the surroundings.

If you have stopped a little on the close side, you will have to teach the pupil how to reverse in a straight line. Use the method described in Chapter 4, but avoid going into too much detail. The finer points of reversing can be added when it is taught as a set exercise later on. As the novice reverses the car be ready to take hold of the wheel if necessary. Many people who are new to reversing have a tendency to wander off course or lose control of the clutch.

CHANGING GEARS

Changing Up

Firstly, explain why the changing of gears is necessary. A way of doing this which is easy to understand is to say that as the speed of the car changes, so does the speed of the engine. To select a higher gear as speed increases and a lower gear as it slows, simply prevents the engine from working too hard. Mention that if the engine is forced to work too hard by being left in a high gear at low speed, it would struggle and possibly stall.

The next task requires a pen and paper. Show your pupil the approximate speed ranges for each gear in the car, rounding the figures up as much as you can to make them easy to remember. So as a rough guide the range for 1st gear may be from zero to a maximum of 15 mph, while for 2nd it may be a minimum of 10 mph up to 25 mph, or whatever the figures may be for your particular vehicle. Point out that what you describe as a maximum is not necessarily the absolute limit to the gear's speed range, but that the car should not be pushed past these points during normal driving conditions.

While the engine is turned off, allow the pupil to go through the positions of the gear lever again to refresh the memory and add a few details:

> *"Make sure your palm is always relaxed and open when moving the lever. Each change should be made smoothly and*

deliberately. Never rush or use force as this can only make things more difficult."

Once they understand this, give theoretical tuition on how to change up.

"Soon after moving off, as the speed of the car increases we will need to change up to second gear. To do this, put the clutch down and at the same time take your foot off the gas. The lever can then be moved to second gear position. I'll talk you through each part of the change when we get moving again. Once the lever is in position, bring the clutch up fully with a nice smooth movement and at the same time go back to the gas. After changing up, we will carry on driving for a short distance before finding somewhere to stop."

The pupil now needs to be given time for a few dry runs. Let them go through the mechanics of the gear change before starting the engine. Instruct them to put the clutch down, select first gear, then to bring the clutch up fully and keep the pedal covered for the moment. Next, tell them to put their right foot over, or near to the gas pedal. This is so that they can move the foot up and down to simulate using the gas -the control itself should not be used during this dry run as the engine may end up flooding and be difficult to start.

If the pupil still has a hand on the gear lever, tell them to put it back on the steering wheel and to imagine they are driving along in first gear, and you are about to change up to second. Before going through the routine, ensure the novice understands that you do not actually want them to use the gas pedal, but just to move their right foot as if it were being operated. Then talk them through the actions.

"Now we're ready to change gear, so it's clutch down, off gas, palm towards me and select second gear."

(You may have to remind them which way to move the lever, especially when the car is on the move.)

"Smoothly bring the clutch up fully and gently Increase the gas, foot away from clutch."

Also, remind them to return the hand to the wheel if necessary. Practise this for as many times as the pupil needs to appear comfortable in making the movements of a gear change, then start the engine and explain that you are going to carry out the same routine but this time while on the move.

Direct your pupil through the procedure for moving off, and once on the move ask for an increase in gas in order to build up sufficient speed. This will have to be a little higher than is really needed as a novice needs several seconds to complete a change in the early stages of practise and the momentum would naturally fall while this is being done. Having attained the correct speed, deliver the instruction:

"Cover the clutch, now ready to change gear," and then continue talking your pupil through the procedure as you did on the dry run.

Before teaching any new skill, do give a proper briefing and ensure the pupil understands what you want them to do. This exercise requires patient instruction from you, as the co-ordination needed in gear changing means that not everyone can pick up the knack easily. Some may need a surprising amount of practise on this alone.

While teaching the use of gears try to be methodical so that things are more likely to be remembered. Start by instructing the beginner to move away and change into second gear, then stop. Repeat the process until you are both happy then move on. Drive away, change up to second gear, then third, and stop. Work up to fourth gear also if possible -this depends on the road space available and the learner's ability.

When changing up to third and fourth, remember to make sure that the driver changes their hand position around to suit the direction of movement.

When changing up has been mastered to some extent, stop for a while and explain that you are going to teach the method for changing down.

Changing Down

"Before changing down, we need to reduce the speed of the car. That means a mirror check must be done before slowing. We can then ease off the gas and also use the brake if we need to lose more speed. Then the clutch is put down and the gear lever can be moved into the position we want. The clutch can then be brought smoothly and fully up, and after a final mirror check we can go back to the gas."

You should teach a novice to complete a gear change down before returning to the gas for a good reason. If braking has been used, the right foot should preferably be kept on, or at least covering, the pedal until the clutch has been fully engaged, as this is really the only way of ensuring a beginner is in control of the speed of the car. This will become vitally important when encountering junctions.

On the move, instruction would be similar to that for changing up. This covers changing down from third to second.

"Shortly we're going to change down to second gear, so check mirrors, ease off the gas, cover brake and cover clutch, gently brake," (if necessary) *"Clutch down, palm towards me, select second gear, smoothly bring the clutch up fully, check mirrors, away from the brake now and gently increase the gas, foot away from clutch."*

When ready, move away working up to third gear, change down to second and stop. Repeat the process until you are both happy, and then give an extra challenge by getting your pupil to pull away and get into third again. Then change down to second, and also into first before coming to a halt. Next, if space and the pupil's ability permit, work up to fourth and all the way back down to first. The use of fourth gear, though, is not essential on the first lesson, and local 20mph speed restrictions sometimes make this impossible anyway.

Although at this point you are teaching the pupil to change down through each gear in turn, you should encourage them to 'block change' when their ability improves. During normal driving, it is quite acceptable, and often preferable to miss out gears, particularly when changing down. There is no point in making three gear changes on approach to a junction for instance when one will do. For the time being though, you should continue to use all the gears to get the pupil used to basic gear changing.

Continuous stopping during this practise session gives the learner chance to relax for a moment or two, and gives you the opportunity to correct any mistakes. Any explanation you attempt to deliver while on the move is unlikely to be understood as a new driver can normally only concentrate on one thing at a time.

After the beginner has grasped the idea of using gears and has no obvious problems, such frequent halts may be unnecessary. They can be kept on the move for longer periods and practise can be concentrated on changing up and down through the gears, in particular between second and third. This is in readiness for junction work.

Try to avoid 'over instruction', after talking them through a gear change or two, if it is obvious that they have picked it up quickly and can carry out the actions without constant prompting then allow them to do so.

Under ideal conditions, gear changing should be taught fully before progressing to other areas, but this is not always possible. In many cases, left turns would have to be covered as well in order to provide the necessary road space. Left turns are dealt with in detail in the next chapter.

GENERAL ADVICE

A lot of theory needs to be explained on the first lesson when dealing with a complete beginner, so the practical side will be shorter than on subsequent sessions. This would, of course, depend on how long the lesson is among other things. Most professional instructors work on a one hour basis which works fine for some learners, whereas many others benefit more from longer drives, more so in the early stages when the pupil needs quite a lot of time to settle down in the driving seat and recall what has gone before.

This first lesson really needs to be 1.5 to 2 hours long. A proper controls lesson ought to take at least 30 minutes, and with the time taken for you to talk about each thing that is covered, most of the first hour will be used up in theory. A second hour gives the novice chance to put theory into practise and this way they are much more likely to retain knowledge until the next lesson.

You will need to keep talking while on the move during these first couple of hours and the following set of early lessons. The sound of your voice is needed to reassure a nervous driver as well as to guide them. When not giving a direct instruction, look well ahead and give the pupil a running commentary on what might affect the drive. Point out probable hazards and try to instil a sense of anticipation. What might be hidden around the next bend or behind the row of parked cars? This will teach a new driver to look well ahead and read the road, enabling them to start formulating a driving plan, something the vast majority of learners - and many experienced drivers - are very weak on. If this is initiated from the very beginning, it will have time to develop before taking to busier areas.

You will spend most of the time on quiet roads until a pupil can exercise good car control, and the transfer to roads carrying heavier traffic must be made as gradually as possible, but you cannot avoid traffic forever. It is essential really to bring about the teaching of road reading as early as this first lesson.

During the first session, most people should be able to handle gear changing and some junction work... although junctions are best avoided if at all possible. Sometimes further progress can be made; or conditions may dictate that hill starts or moving off at an angle must be taught. But try not to overload a new pupil with more than they can handle. Keep things fairly simple at such an early stage.

The amount of progress that each person makes can be radically different. I have encountered the occasional pupil who can be taught every set exercise in three or four lessons, and is practically ready for test after 10 or 12 hours. But on the other side of the fence I recall one individual, a little on the slow side, who tried my patience for over three hours before getting successfully into second gear! After six hours tuition we made it up to third gear and back down to second, and a further seven hours later we negotiated the first correct left turn! These, though, are exceptions that clearly show the difference in people's capabilities. A good instructor must tailor themselves to the pupil and exercise the patience of a saint when necessary.

If you are unlucky enough to have a pupil like my young friend, who, despite much practise and pushing cannot seem to make any progress, do not start putting them down and telling them how useless they are... it could be your lack of skill that is to blame! If you really have given all and got nowhere over a period of lessons, the best way is to leave the job to a professional.

With patience and expertise a problem learner can sometimes be crafted into an above average driver. This happened with the difficult pupil mentioned earlier. Twice I suggested that he might find driving an automatic less of a challenge, to which he replied:

"No, I know I'm a bit daft but I just want you to keep hammering it into me!"

What could I say to that? Needless to say I kept hammering, and can very proudly recall that after over 60 hours tuition he passed the test at the second attempt. Towards the latter part of his course of lessons he became one of the safest and most attentive pupils I have ever taught.

Perseverance and dogged resilience are needed when at times you may feel like giving up. But when people like this do reach the standard and pass the test you can look back with pride and congratulate yourself for a job well done. It can be a great feeling, sometimes from sheer relief!

Whatever happens on the first lesson, it is rarely a clear indication of how things are going to progress. Some will seem to be going along nicely but will grind to a halt when they find an inability to reverse. Others start off badly or flounder at the half-way stage and then everything suddenly clicks into place.

A popular question for professional instructors is *'How many lessons will I need?'* There is simply no way of telling. How many lessons you will have to give your learner depends on many factors: age, co-ordination, how much they understand about cars and driving before getting into the driving seat, how regular lessons are, and your teaching ability. Nothing can be taken for granted.

ENDING THE LESSON

At the end of each lesson you will need to have a little time to spare for discussion. Point out areas where extra practise is needed, give praise and encouragement where it has been earned and make the pupil feel that they have achieved something. It is also an opportune time to test your learner's knowledge of driving. Ask a few questions on the Highway Code and get them to identify or describe some road signs. At the conclusion of the session, give your novice something to look forward to by letting them know what they will be doing next time, and advise them to study the Highway Code or Driving Manual to see what they can find on this subject before the following lesson.

THE FOLLOWING LESSON

If all has gone reasonably well on the first lesson, the novice can move off and stop successfully and change up and down through the gears; the next step will be to move on to teach junctions. If there have been problems though, do not attempt to progress on to a different subject. Always practise what has been done on previous lessons and ensure the learner has a reasonable command of everything that has been covered before setting new goals.

I cannot set out a programme where the learner is taught junctions on the second lesson and reversing on the fifth, or whatever the intervals may be... people are too individual for that. The skills to be learned by the pupil are laid out in order throughout this book, although they cannot always be followed in strict sequence. Your job is to make sure that the novice can carry out each exercise fairly well before being allowed to attempt anything new.

3
APPROACHING JUNCTIONS

Junctions are hazards which will very likely be encountered during the first lesson after the new driver has learned moving off and stopping and perhaps an amount of gear changing. Initially the novice should only be taught left turns and an area where successive left turns can be made without meeting a main road needs to be found. Before the pupil is taken through the approach to junctions, however, another skill should be covered - clutch control.

CLUTCH CONTROL

A beginner will often find their judgement of speed and stopping distances far from perfect and will probably end up halting well short of the give way lines when approaching junctions, resulting in being in a position from which proper visibility cannot be obtained. Creeping forward for a better view under clutch control is the only answer.

To practise clutch control, park on a stretch of road which is clear for some distance and explain what you are going to do. Get the pupil ready to drive and talk them through the normal preparations for moving off. When a safe opportunity arises, instruct your pupil to keep the feet still and release the parking brake. Hopefully the car will begin to move slowly forward, if not, as with the moving off procedure ask the driver carefully to bring the clutch up a fraction and then remind them to:

"Keep feet still."

Aim for a very low speed and if necessary instruct the novice to put the clutch a fraction down in order to maintain a snail's pace. When a slow and steady speed has been achieved, instruct:

"Keep your left foot still on the clutch now, but give the engine a little more gas."

If they do manage to keep the clutch still there will be no increase in speed despite the extra power. The pupil should be made to notice this, proving that against what they probably believed, the gas pedal does not control the rate of acceleration when first moving from rest. The point can then be pressed home by asking them to bring the clutch up smoothly and the car will accelerate.

Let them practise this several times; all the time being careful to keep things safe by keeping your eyes on what is happening around the car. Have your driver creep forward to a specific point before lifting the clutch fully as if to drive away, but then get them to stop and repeat the exercise. When you can see that they are well in control of the idea, your attention can be turned to the matter of making a few left turns.

TURNING LEFT

Before briefing your pupil on how to make a left turn, park within sight of a junction, this can then be referred to as the explanation is made. A prepared diagram or a drawing as you teach will help a great deal in making your learner understand the manoeuvre.

The process of turning left is simple enough to the experienced driver but not to most beginners. Here they are asked to do not one action, such as setting off, where preparations are made while the vehicle is stationary, but to co-ordinate a series of actions in sequence while the car is on the move. At first this is a daunting prospect for some, therefore we don't want to complicate things too much. A novice driver may only be able to cope with using first and second gears if junctions are fairly close together and should be kept at quite a low speed to begin with. But if you have a more capable pupil or the junctions are well spaced out, third gear should also be used.

One of the first things to point out is that there are two basic types of turn: into a side or minor road and on to a major road where one has to give way to passing or approaching traffic. Note here that a major road is not necessarily a main road; it is simply one which has priority over a side turning. You must also explain the three ways of indicating that the give way rule applies: the double broken white line, the inverted white triangle painted on the road, and at busier junctions, the upright give way sign may also be seen.

During the early practise of left turns, it is good policy to get the pupil to stop each time they encounter give way lines. This gives them ample time to look before emerging, and it will also help further the practise of moving off and stopping. Although if you have a clear view on the approach and someone is close behind you, then it may be safer to make the turn without stopping. Explain this to your pupil before going through the approach routine.

The approach itself can sometimes be a matter for improvisation, but you must first lay down the basic guidelines.

Turning Left into a Side Road

On the approach to a turn, Mirror checks are of course the first priority, followed normally by an indicator Signal -'M S'. Next consideration is Position, which for a left turn would not usually mean any deviation from the normal driving line. Speed must then be reduced and where necessary a lower Gear needs to be selected (unless you are already in second gear) -'P S G'. Then just before turning there must be a final mirror check, a check on anything else that may be approaching the same junction, and a good Look into the side road itself -'L'. The arrows shown on the diagram (Fig. 3) represent the three points of observation.

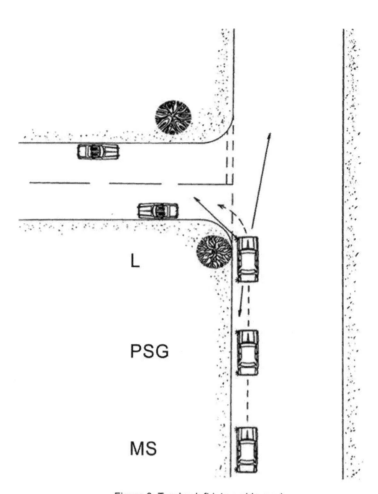

Figure 3. Turning left into a side road

So the full sequence, which is carried out for all junctions, is: Mirrors, Signal, Position, Speed, Gear, Look (MS-PSG-L).

The look into the side road is one part of the sequence which will need further explanation; you may meet parked cars and oncoming traffic. The pupil must be informed of what to do in this instance. Parked cars on their own shouldn't prove much of a problem, except for the fact that if one is on your side you will have to take a wider course in order to give it 'adequate clearance'. Difficulties can arise though when there is also something travelling towards you.

If you are to drive through a gap between a parked car and another one on the move, there must be a minimum clearance of about three feet either side. A new driver may have difficulty in judging this gap so the decision whether to continue or wait has to be yours. If the other driver sees you coming they will sometimes wait for you if they are courteous, but you have no guarantee. If you are in any doubt whatsoever, instruct the pupil to stop before completing the turn so that the other vehicle can emerge safely. You can then move off again with more space available. Ensure your novice understands the golden rule in situations like this: If in doubt, stop.

Pedestrians crossing the side road can also complicate an otherwise straightforward left turn. Forewarn the driver of what to do but always be ready to step in yourself if the pupil shows no sign of reacting to the problem. Inexperienced newcomers can very easily be panicked by the presence of people crossing or about to cross the road they are going to enter.

You have two options to follow when pedestrians are encountered:

1. Stop before beginning the turn in order to allow the people time to cross

2. If the pedestrian is a little way from the road edge and showing no obvious signs of looking round before

crossing, instruct the pupil to give a light warning tap on the horn or do this yourself if it is within reach and the pupil is slow to react. The people will then hopefully stop and turn round, giving you time to turn safely. Always give a wave of thanks as you pass!

Some will ignore the horn or react improperly to it, especially immature youths and children, so with these you have to be extra careful. Even after sounding the horn stopping may still be necessary; it does not give you right of way and could escape the notice of someone who is hard of hearing. There are also plenty of people stupid enough to ignore the warning even when it is in the interest of their own safety.

The horn and headlamp flasher are, I think, the two most misused instruments in the car. Teach your student when and when not to use them from the very beginning.

Turning Left onto a Major Road

The pupil may be informed that the approach sequence to a major road is basically the same as that used for a minor road, (Fig. 4). The only difference is at the final approach when, in addition to the last mirror checks, observation must be regular looks to the right and left. Remind them that they may be stopping at the give way lines even though it may be safe to emerge, and some steering to the left needs to be done just before halting.

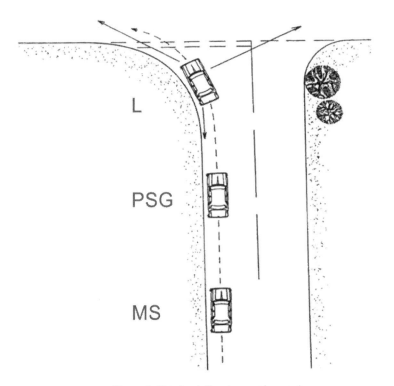

Figure 4. Turning left onto a major road

Variations in the routine

The approach to a junction has six basic features, but this series of events cannot always be carried out in strict order. For instance, there is little point in checking mirrors and signalling left if you are then forced out to the right because of a parked car near the corner. The only option is to move out and reduce speed before signalling left.

Or alternatively, on the approach to a major road you cannot signal left before slowing down if there is a minor road to the left near the end with a vehicle waiting to emerge. This would again be regarded as an incorrect signal which might be misinterpreted by the driver waiting to emerge as an indication that you were intending to turn into their road. In this situation, following traffic will expect you to slow down anyway because of the junction ahead and the signal can be delayed until you are passing the side road.

You need to show the pupil the basic pattern of approach as described earlier, then explain that there may be some variation when additional hazards are met at or near the junction. Use a pen and paper to draw a few examples such as those I've given, this will help avoid any confusion to the learner if you have to change the sequence of in instructions while on the move.

Practising Left Turns

Now comes the hard part, putting theory into practise and getting on the move again. Not only has the novice more to think about now, so have you; this is where your job starts to get harder.

Total instruction will still be needed for most new drivers and you must allow time for this. You need time to decide on the right course of action at any hazard and to deliver the instructions, and the pupil needs time to react and carry them out. Keeping your learner to a slow enough speed to cope with this is essential. Through previous practise they should be able to change gear on their own but will probably lack the judgement to tell when and where gear changes need to be carried out. This is why, as mentioned earlier, you may need to restrict use of gears to first and second initially.

The importance of keeping directions clear must again be stressed here. If you want the pupil to take the next road on the left say:

"I want you to take the next road on the left," and then instruct, or:

"At the end I want you to turn left."

A casual remark like 'turn left at the end' could well have you in someone's driveway before you even finish the sentence!

INSTRUCTION ON THE MOVE

Left into a Side Road

Having safely set off and selected second gear, the pupil now needs to be guided up to and through the left turn. Once the driver has been directed give the relevant orders:

"Check mirrors, indicate down for left." (Many people do forget which way the indicator lever should be moved).

"Keeping to your normal position, check mirrors, ease off the gas, look ahead and into the junction."

At the corner:

"Steer to the left now, look well ahead and straighten the steering, check mirrors and gently increase the gas."

Common mistakes are going back to the gas too soon and poor judgement of the steering. If the novice does try to accelerate too early, repeat the former instruction:

"Ease off the gas," and add *"Wait till we get through the corner."*

Steering errors can be prevented simply by telling the beginner when to start turning and when to straighten up as part of the normal instruction. But if your pupil begins drifting too close to the kerb or too wide, don't hesitate to take control of the wheel yourself to put the car on to a safe line.

If a stop might be anticipated due to a blind corner, oncoming traffic or pedestrians, when you instruct ease off the gas, you should also add:

"Cover brake and cover clutch," so that both pedals are ready for instant use. If you manage to carry on without actually halting, after straightening up direct the driver:

"Away from the brake now and gently increase the gas, foot away from clutch."

This approach can gradually be modified as the learner gains more experience to the stage where they can drive the car all the way through the corner under gentle acceleration. This may not need any instruction from you as often they will reach this point naturally in their own time without having to be told.

Left onto a Major Road

Approaching a major road, direct the pupil in good time and remind them of your intention to stop at the give way lines unless someone is close behind you and you can easily see that it is clear to continue. This time we will include a parked car to complicate things a little:

"There is a parked car near the junction so check mirrors, and while it's clear move out to the right and ease off the gas. Indicate down for left, cover brake and cover clutch. Check mirrors and keep looking both ways, steer to the left, gently

braking and clutch down as you stop at the lines. Keep your feet still."

If the road is level you need only talk through the procedure for moving off again, but if there is any suspicion of a slope the parking brake must be applied, the gas set, and the clutch brought to biting point. When you are ready to move on again, in addition to the normal right-left-right looks; ensure the pupil takes a final mirror check, particularly in the left-hand door mirror. In the time it takes you to get ready, a cyclist could easily have come up alongside you.

In this approach sequence there are 12 separate instructions, so you can see why time is needed for them all to be given and carried out, and why it may be necessary to miss out the use of third gear. Third gear should be brought in if junctions are a fair distance apart but don't expect a novice to make a quick change on the final approach. If you need to talk them through the change down it will have to be made earlier than would normally be the case in order to leave time for the final preparations.

You may have noticed that no signal was given to the right before moving out for the parked car. Some people encourage learners to indicate every time this is done... an unnecessary and irritating habit. If you are following another vehicle and there is a parked car ahead, in the absence of a pulling in signal, the fact that you will move out to pass it will be obvious. Any driver who continually signals right in this situation will eventually mislead other road users into thinking they are going to turn right. When there is a side road to the right with another vehicle waiting to emerge, that unnecessary signal could be assessed as a potential danger, definitely so if the other vehicle emerges.

EMERGING AT JUNCTIONS

An important thing to remember as you approach and emerge from these junctions is that technically, you are in control of the car. Whether it be verbally or by direct action using the parking brake and steering wheel, sounding the horn or operating the indicators if need be, make sure you keep the vehicle safe.

Don't expect a novice to make decisions as to when it is safe to proceed. This is your responsibility during the early steps into driving. Get yourself into a seating position that enables you to see clearly and move in the seat when you have to, to obtain a proper view. The pupil will often fail to notice cyclists and small mopeds. They will look for large vehicles which could seemingly pose a threat, but often appear to miss or ignore the two-wheeler tucked into the kerbside. The danger here is that because of the driver's head and torso blocking your view, the cyclist or moped rider is often hidden from your gaze unless you lean back or forth to eliminate the blind area.

As well as taking full observation yourself, the pupil must also be watched to check that they are taking proper observation before emerging. On left turns, they will often exhibit a habit for only looking to the right and ignoring the possibility of parked cars and oncoming traffic from the left. (It's strange how many faults are shared by learners and experienced motorists who let standards drop after passing the test!) A sure sign that this is happening is when the beginner fails to keep the car on a proper course as they start to move off. They may come too close to the kerb, but more often will allow the vehicle to drift wide.

Another great weakness of many novices is in their inability to judge speed. As they are going along at a nice steady 10 - 20 mph they may not realise that other traffic is probably travelling much faster. You must decide when it is safe to carry on and keep the pupil informed so that they can understand why each decision is made and learn from this.

When several left turns have been carried out, stop for a short break and discuss any faults that are evident. These should then be worked upon until an improvement is achieved. Turning left needs to be practised until your student is able to complete two or three circuits without any real problems occurring. When this standard has been reached you may progress on to right turns.

TURNING RIGHT

Turning right is potentially one of the most dangerous driving manoeuvres. Positioning is much more difficult and more care needs to be taken with observation. This exercise usually poses more problems for the beginner as there are many more opportunities for making errors.

If right turns are being taught at the start of a new lesson, give the pupil a few left turns to begin with to warm up and help settle them down - it is always a good idea to practise what has gone before. After the warm up, turn the car round yourself if necessary in order to use the same circuit of turns but in the opposite direction if this is practicable. If not, drive to a more suitable venue. As with left turns, park within sight of the first turn you intend to make.

The briefing should follow along the same lines as that used for turning left, but this time it is of particular importance to stress the rules of correct positioning.

Turning Right onto a Major Road

The approach sequence is basically the same as that used for turning left, the signal and position, of course, being the differing factor (Fig. 5). Show the pupil that after the mirrors are used and the right-turn signal is given, the position should be taken up which normally means moving to just left of the centre-line. But explain that this is not always done. On fairly narrow roads the car must remain on the left to leave room for other vehicles that may be turning in.

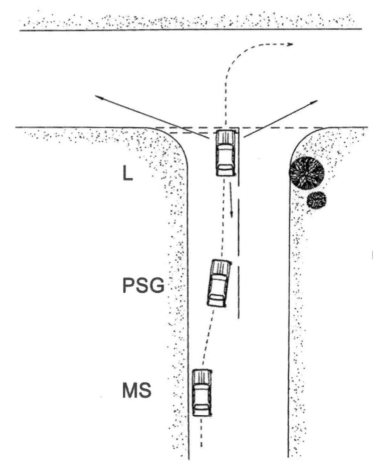

Figure 5. Turning right onto a major road

On the move this is something you will have to look out for. Many drivers do have a tendency to move to the right automatically even when, on a narrow road, their wheels are already left of centre. You must also remember and point out that a line of parked cars along the right-hand side of the street can turn an otherwise normal width road into a narrow lane

(Fig. 6). Moving over to the right here can create a very small if not impassable gap to oncoming traffic.

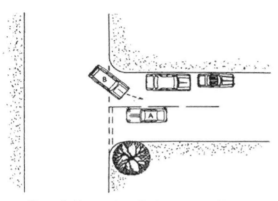

Figure 6. Upper - Car 'A' takes up a position near to the centre line and prevents car 'B' from entering the road.

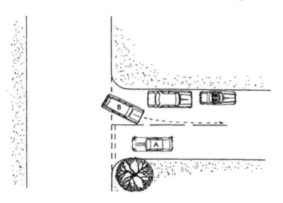

Figure 6. Lower - Car 'A' keeps more to the left and leaves room for car 'B' to turn safely.

On roads where sufficient space is available to move over to the right, ensure that this is not done blindly. After the normal mirror checks and signal, rear observation must be taken again particularly using the right-hand door mirror before moving over. When you are being followed by another vehicle, even after indicating right there is no guarantee that an impatient driver will not attempt to pass you before reaching the junction, more so when the new driver is travelling at what the other motorist may consider to be an unnecessarily slow speed.

So now the learner knows how to position on approach, but what happens at the junction itself? A common fault among all drivers is turning too early and encroaching on to the wrong side of the road. If something appears after you have partly emerged and you are forced to stop, the car is then in a position which narrows the opening making it very difficult for the approaching vehicle to enter the side road should the driver wish to do so (Fig. 7).

To avoid this, instruct your pupil that when they move on again from the junction, they must refrain from steering until they begin to cross the give-way lines. Just how far forward will depend on the width of the road you are entering. You must exercise your own judgement on this and guide the novice's steering movements through your instructions while on the move.

Sometimes though you may find a parked obstruction directly opposite the junction; the result of a thoughtless, lazy driver who cannot manage to walk a few yards from a safe parking place. In this case, the steering would naturally have to begin earlier to ensure adequate clearance is given to the other vehicle as you emerge. When this happens, keep the pupil informed as to why things must be done a little differently.

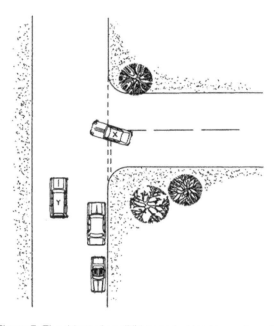

Figure 7. The driver of car 'X' began turning too early and had to stop when driver 'Y' came into view. Driver 'Y' now has a very difficult turn to make and will probably have to stop and wait.

Turning Right into a Side Road

Turning from a major road into a side road, the same rules on positioning govern the approach; left of centre on roads where space is available, keeping more to the left when the road is narrow (Fig. 8.)

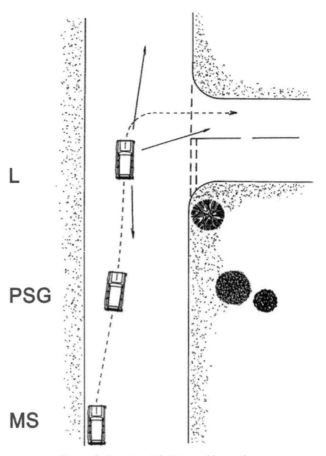

Figure 8. Turning right into a side road

The same advice on pedestrians crossing the junction and traffic emerging from the road as given for left turns should be followed. The main difference with this type of turn is the likelihood of oncoming traffic. Explain that any vehicles approaching have priority over you in this instance and must be allowed to pass before you complete the right turn. However, ensure the pupil understands that, if the way is clear or there is a safe gap in any approaching traffic, the turn may be carried out without stopping.

If you need to give way, instruct that the car must be brought to a halt with its front level with or just before the centre of the side road, and that this is the point at which the turn should begin. Turning at the centre-line is to make sure the corner is not 'cut' as you turn.

If a corner is cut when the view into the road is restricted (Fig. 9a), or the road is narrowed by parked cars near the junction (Fig. 9b), the error would certainly be serious or even dangerous. The only time a corner should be cut is when there are parked cars etc. on the left-hand side of the minor road which are very close to the mouth of the junction (Fig. 9c). In this case, the corner has to be cut in order to give adequate clearance to the obstruction but should still be done with a great deal of caution.

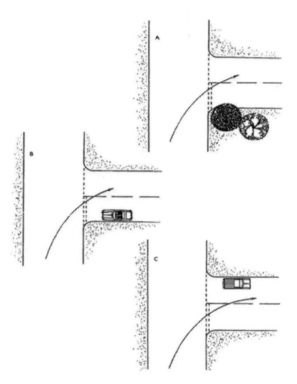

Figure 9. Cutting a corner should only be done when there is no alternative (9c), both 9a and 9b are avoidable.

Turning into a side road on the right can prove to be the most troublesome turn for many new drivers, often because of the possible or actual approach of other traffic whose path may have to be crossed. When a vehicle does appear, a timid driver will stare transfixed at it and forget all about the road they were supposed to be entering. The result of this is usually late steering and missing the turning point.

This can be helped by making sure the pupil is taking proper observation into the road as well as looking ahead. If you do over-run the target you may have to consider driving on to the next junction if one is available or, if you have a fairly wide opening, the turn could be attempted but be careful of people behind you. There are some drivers stupid enough to pass you on your right to beat you into the side road. This does happen occasionally and you must be ready to take control of the steering if the novice shows any sign of losing control of the wheel.

Practising Right Turns

Advice for right turns is basically the same as that given for left turns; a quiet area must be chosen where you will not meet conditions which would prove difficult for a novice driver. Preferably the roads used for the first few right turns should be fairly wide so as to make steering and positioning less of a problem.

INSTRUCTION ON THE MOVE

Right onto a Major Road

The first turn we are going to make is on to a major road. The road is of reasonable width and the approach is clear.

"At the end of the road I want you to turn right. Remember we are intending to stop at the lines. Check mirrors, indicate up for right. Check mirrors again and move over near to the centre-line. Ease off the gas cover brake and cover clutch, check mirrors and keep looking both ways, gently brake, clutch down and stop at the lines. Keep your feet still."

The trick now is in getting the pupil to control the clutch properly as they set off again. Assume now that the road is level, we have changed into first gear and the major road is clear.

"Set the gas, check mirrors and look both ways. Slowly bring the clutch up until the car moves. Now feet still and look both ways again, feet still and steer quickly to the right. Steer back to your normal position now, smoothly bring the clutch up fully. Check mirrors and gently increase the gas, foot away from clutch."

The second look both ways will give time for the vehicle to move to the correct turning point before steering begins, and the two reminders to 'keep feet still' should hopefully keep the clutch under control.

Right into a Minor Road

The next turn is into a side road where parked cars are on the right on the approach, and we will also include an oncoming car.

"I want you to take the next road on the right. It's just after the line of parked cars. Check mirrors. Indicate up for right but keep to your normal position because the other cars make the road narrow."

If the learner does start to move to the right, pull the wheel gently back and repeat: *"Keep to your normal position"*.

"There is an approaching car so we may have to stop. Check mirrors, ease off the gas, cover brake and cover clutch, now keep looking ahead and into the junction."

If you can turn comfortably before or after the vehicle then do so, but if you are in any doubt about the space available, inform the pupil that you are going to stop when level with the centre-line of the side road, and talk them through the stopping procedure.

It may be that you could continue by slowing right down, selecting first gear while on the move, and turning just after the other car has passed but this may be too hard for most novices at such an early stage. So even though it takes a few seconds longer, stop and wait for a decent gap. If there is any further oncoming traffic don't push your trainee into making any turn hurriedly, even if people are waiting behind you. They will need time to control the car properly and must be allowed to make the turn at a leisurely pace until skill improves.

Having stopped, prepare the pupil for moving on again. Use the parking brake if the wait is for more than a few seconds or there is a gradient. We will assume, however, that the road is level and the wait a short one. When the wait is for a longer period, remind your student to keep looking into the road as well as watching oncoming traffic as the situation may change. Pedestrians may arrive who want to cross the road or another vehicle may come along the side road preventing you from entering. When you are prepared for setting off and the way is clear, instruct:

"We are safe to turn now so check mirrors and set the gas, slowly bring the clutch up till the car moves then keep your feet still and steer quickly to the right. Straighten your steering now, smoothly bring the clutch up fully, check mirrors and gently increase the gas, foot away from clutch."

If you were able to make the same turn without halting, perhaps after the oncoming vehicle had passed, give instruction along these lines:

"After the car has passed we will be clear to turn so check mirrors and keep the looks going. Ease off the gas and cover brake to let the car pass. Now as we near the centre-line look well down the road and steer quickly to the right. Straighten your steering now, check mirrors, away from the brake and gently Increase the gas."

STEERING FAULTS

Problems with steering are very common among new drivers, nervous ones in particular, because of a tendency to grip the wheel too tightly or a reluctance to release the wheel with one hand while the other pulls or pushes. This will be more evident on right turns where steering needs to be done faster.

Where a driver does have a control problem, there are exercises which can be carried out to improve steering technique. The very tense beginner could benefit from a simple practise routine.

All you need to do is to get the pupil to drive along with just one hand on the wheel for a distance, making sure, of course, that there are no sharp bends ahead. Repeat this using the opposite hand for a similar amount of time. This should help convince the learner that the wheel does not have to be gripped tightly by both hands whenever the vehicle is moving. Practise this as much as you think is necessary before returning to junction work, and mention to the pupil that driving with one hand should not become a habit!

Another solution is to carry out a series of 'figure eights' where space permits. Find a large open area, such as an empty car park, and demonstrate how easily the car can be steered when the wheel is turned in full half circles, so the hands touch at top and bottom each time the movement is made. Turn the wheel on to full left lock and then quickly change to full right lock in order to cover the figure of eight shape. Let your student practise this until they can steer rapidly while still appearing to look comfortable at the wheel.

These exercises should go a long way to improving performance and control of the steering and can be used whenever necessary if the pupil continues to exhibit faults in this area.

THE NEXT STAGE OF JUNCTION PRACTISE

Once some mastery of car control has developed, junctions can be taken on to the next stage. Rather than stopping at the give way lines each time, the learner may be allowed to carry on if the way is clear. Before doing this, more emphasis needs to be placed on the importance of correct and effective observation before emerging.

Effective observation does not just mean looking right, left and right again, but looking early enough and for long enough to be able to judge accurately what any traffic on the major road is doing. The golden rules of emerging state that you must not cause vehicles to slow down or to change direction in order to avoid you as you emerge.

When other traffic is approaching, before crossing the give way point you must have time to make three decisions: How far away is the vehicle, how fast is it coming and how quickly can you pull away yourself? An inexperienced driver cannot work this out in fractions of a second. That's why speed on approach and length of time spent looking are so important, they need time to assess the situation properly. Your pupil must be made aware of these factors before attempting to drive on at a junction without stopping.

Attention should also be brought to 'zones of vision' with relative speed on approach, in other words the more restricted the view is on the approach to a junction, the slower the speed must be in order to give more time for observation. Explain that there may be many junctions where a clear view cannot be obtained even when you have reached the give way lines, a 'blind junction'. Tell your pupil that at these junctions you will make a stop at the lines as usual for the time being.

You can now begin coming up to junctions with the intention of carrying on if the way is clear, but remember, the decision as to whether to drive on or stop must still be made by you at this stage, and if you are in any doubt, instruct your pupil to stop.

Practise driving on with left turns first, then reintroduce turning to the right. If there are no apparent problems, the drive can then become more varied. To add interest and more of a challenge, inform the student that you are going to start doing turns at random. You will give your directions in plenty of time but the turns will be a mixture of junctions to the left and right. Make sure you plan these turns well in advance and you must still remain within the quiet practise area and not wander out on to a main road!

How much a learner driver can be pushed along depends, of course, on the Individual's ability, but before considering taking them from quiet roads out into a little traffic, you must be satisfied that a reasonable degree of car control has been attained, and that the driver is capable of making progress at a speed which will not unduly hinder other road users. For this reason the approach to junctions needs to be modified a little further.

When you arrive at a blind junction, stopping every time when the major road might well be clear of traffic is not the best way of making good progress. Where a gradient is present no matter how small, the parking brake then has to be used and preparations for a hill start carried out, further hindering progress and putting extra pressure on your pupil when other people may be waiting behind. They will learn to deal with this in due course but it is better for all concerned if it can be avoided by not actually stopping in the first place.

It may take a lot of practise for some, but all learners must be taught to change down to first gear while on the move and to adapt this to junctions. At the point just before coming to rest, first gear can be selected and the clutch brought up just high enough to keep the vehicle moving very slowly. The beginner can then learn how to creep forward under clutch control to a position where vision is unobstructed and from there a decision can be made to carry on or stop. If you are forced to halt in a partially emerged position the parking brake should be applied - most roads are cambered and once over the lines you are effectively going uphill.

Arguments are frequently waged over the subject of the parking brake: when the car stops for a short while should it be applied or not? Some people seem to think that there is one rule for a learner and everyone else can do what they like. In my opinion the parking brake is an indispensable safety device which should be set whenever the vehicle comes to a halt, unless the stop is only for a few seconds and the road is on the level. This applies to experienced motorists and learners alike.

During a beginner's first few hours of practise, each stop they make at a junction will only be for a few moments anyway as the area you take them to will be very quiet. For these the parking brake need not be used providing the road is not on an incline. But as you gradually merge into busier traffic the waiting will increase and use of the parking brake must be encouraged. Without this I guarantee that your pupil will be rolling back at some stage. You may well advise that the brake should be set for a hill start, but all it takes sometimes is the camber of the road to provide a 'hill' and here the novice may not even recognise the fact that they are on a gradient. So at junctions and all other places where a stop is more than a few seconds long, even an absolute beginner can manage to use the parking brake. Teach this from an early stage and it will stick!

So normal road junctions then can be tackled in three stages, but let me stress at this point that each part does not represent a new lesson, nor must all three stages be covered before teaching anything other than junctions. A trainee may be brought to the second stage and kept there for a few lessons, perhaps while the emergency stop is introduced or maybe some reversing.

Once good clutch control is established after a little reversing experience the third stage of junctions could be started. Even with many of my better pupils I have found that this first gear approach can pose a few difficulties and more often than not a practical demonstration has to be given to show how to time each movement. This latter stage does require a fair degree of control and confidence and it is important not to attempt the most difficult part of junction work too early.

CROSSROADS

While teaching junctions, the area you are practising in may not be as perfect as might be desired and you might well have to deal with crossroads. These will, in all probability, still be quiet if the venue has been chosen wisely, but it will mean having to discuss rules of priority here in addition to the normal approach procedure.

At some point you are almost certain to encounter this little problem... having taught the novice the priority rules at crossroads, you are coming up to one with the intention of turning right. An approaching vehicle is at the far side of the junction and as no signal is showing you assume that they are coming straight on into your road. You remind the pupil that the oncoming car has priority over you because of this. The other driver then stops at the give way lines and flashes their lights or waves you on. What do you do now?

If you seem to show a reluctance to turn first, the opposing driver will often lose patience and set off just as you start moving, then everyone is in trouble. Other drivers frequently think that despite the L plates, your student driver should be able to think and act as quickly as they would in the same situation; yet you may not be able to get your pupil to move off immediately. Their reactions may not be that fast yet, they may be confused and, after all, what does the Highway Code say about the flashing of headlights? (I bet you don't know without having to resort to looking at the Code!)

The first thing to do is to take the time you and your pupil need and don't be panicked into rushing. Providing you check all around to ensure it is safe, you could wave the other driver on instead, but be careful. If the view is not great or they act on your signal by pulling out without looking (and people do) they may blame you if something goes wrong.

Otherwise, if you are sure they are intent on waiting, acknowledge this with a wave of thanks, but while the pupil is being readied for moving away keep your hand showing. This should then be interpreted by the other driver that you have not forgotten them and they should wait while you are giving the relevant instructions. They ought to be able to see that you are attempting to get your pupil moving, but you may still find that the other driver loses patience and drives on anyway, be ready to take quick action if necessary should this happen.

It would help all concerned if people refrained from these annoying 'courtesies' in the first place. They seem to think they are doing you a favour when, in fact, it complicates things needlessly and puts unwanted pressure on the new driver. No one, while learning to drive, enjoys being watched by other people. Take note yourself please; if you come across a learner who is at a junction or doing some kind of manoeuvre, carry on if you can do so safely. The best way to help, is to get out of the way!

If this does happen be sure to stop after the incident and explain things fully to the pupil. Please warn them against the misuse of their own headlight flasher in future, as it can and does cause accidents sometimes when interpreted by others as a signal to go ahead when it may not be safe.

ROUNDABOUTS

Ideally, after a novice has demonstrated a good grasp of junction work and car control, driving into a little light traffic and tackling roundabouts is the step which should be taken next, if you are fortunate enough to have a few quiet ones nearby. If the only available roundabouts in the vicinity are busy, these should be avoided. You have a choice of taking the trainee to another area or leaving this type of junction until the pupil has gained more experience.

Roundabouts to most experienced drivers are a fairly easy type of junction to negotiate. You simply watch for a suitable gap in the traffic flow and adjust the approach speed to coincide with it - easy. Isn't it? Not to the majority of new drivers.

To the novice, a junction like this appears to take on the complexities of a maze from which there is no escape, and often no entrance! Although the approach seems straightforward enough, a lot of observation and decision making has to be carried out before arriving at the give way point. The driver must begin observation from well back and as circulation of traffic through the junction is continually monitored, they must be thinking all the time whether to maintain speed or reduce it, which gear to use and whether any vehicles waiting to enter the roundabout are going to set off and prevent them from entering the junction. All this, an experienced motorist will take as a matter of course, but a beginner's main weakness is lack of planning.

Rather than looking well ahead and formulating a plan to fit in with what is happening in the roundabout, they tend to concentrate on reducing the momentum and changing down through the gears, leaving observation until the final run up. By this time their speed may be so slow that they will miss gaps which could otherwise have been taken.

Lack of proper signalling from other drivers does not make life easier for the learner. It is really down to the experience of the instructor to guide the pupil and to navigate a safe course up to and through the roundabout.

Before wandering into the potential confusion of roundabouts, the learner requires a full and detailed briefing. If possible park within sight of a roundabout so the pupil can watch the principles you are teaching being put into practise. This needs the co-operation of other drivers to be doing things correctly! You can then set to work explaining what to do. To assist in making things clear for the novice, this is one subject for which the use of explanatory diagrams is a must.

Point out the signs and road markings which may be found at roundabouts and ensure the pupil knows which way to go round. It may seem absurd that some people will not be aware of which way traffic circulates in this type of junction but believe me there is always one who will go anti-clockwise when asked to turn right!

Priority can be explained by telling the driver that whichever direction they intend to take, they may enter the roundabout when they can do so without making traffic coming from the right slow down or change direction. Roundabouts are designed to keep traffic flowing and when properly used are a relatively easy way of leaving one road to join another.

To save time on the briefing, it helps if the pupil has some prior knowledge of the subject. You should insist that they study the theory of roundabouts in the Highway Code or Driving manual before the lesson. It is a good idea to do this for all lessons really when you are going to teach a particular subject. Most people should be familiar with what to do at a standard three exit roundabout, but what about a more complex junction like the one in Fig. 10?

To leave by the first exit is simple enough and obviously classed as a left turn, but what about the second exit? (Ask the pupil what course they would take). It is also leading off to the left but clearly we cannot signal left on the approach and must delay the exit signal until passing the first road. The same would apply, of course, for the 'road ahead' - exit three. Roads four and five are to be treated as right turns.

To summarise the basic rules, the first exit from a roundabout can generally be classed as a left turn (although on occasions the first road may be literally straight on). Any exit between the first and the 12 o'clock point of the island should be treated as a 'road ahead' (keep to the left and signal left when passing the previous exit), while exits past this point should be approached as right turns.

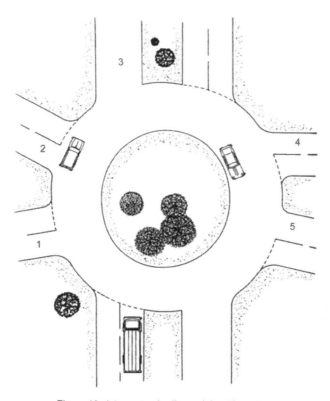

Figure 10. A 'non-standard' roundabout layout

There will be roundabouts in your area where things may have to be done quite differently owing to road marking and layouts; your local knowledge of the area will equip you to deal with any irregularities.

Turning Left at a Roundabout

When turning left at a roundabout, the approach is generally similar to the method of turning left you and your learner have been practising for normal junctions. The 'MS-PSG-L' routine still needs to be put into practise and the same goes for when you are intending to take any other exit from the junction. The only real difference is that on roundabouts the corner you are turning may be gentler than it would be at a T-Junction or crossroads, and the view is usually much better.

For this reason, if you have a confident and capable pupil it may be possible to maintain a slightly higher speed and perhaps remain in third gear to go through some junctions. Inform your student that this may be possible at many of the larger roundabouts. On relatively small islands, however, or where you are in doubt about the view available, speed should be slower and a lower gear selected for the approach.

Point out that although they must keep checking to the right for an opportunity to enter the roundabout, all-round observations must not be neglected. They also need to make sure that they have a clear path through the roundabout and are aware of what may lie at the exit, in case there is something which may prevent them from accelerating away (queuing traffic, people, zebra crossings).

Taking the Road Ahead

Planning to take the 'road ahead' (Fig. 11) which could be any exit between the first and 12 o'clock point, requires a little more thought. As well as searching for a gap in the roundabout itself the driver also has to select the appropriate lane before arrival at the junction. You will of course, inform the pupil which lane to use well in advance. Show the novice the type of lane markings that may be used and remind them that in the absence of any lane arrows the rule is to keep to the left hand lane, and that whichever lane is used on the approach should be maintained until the exit.

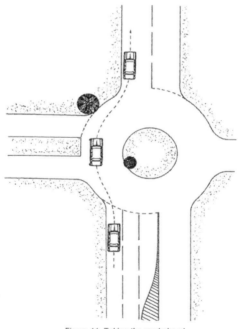

Figure 11. Taking the road ahead

Although no signal is needed before entering the roundabout when taking the road ahead, give a reminder that the mirrors must still be used as the first part of the approach sequence, some tend to associate mirrors only with signals and may neglect them otherwise. Observation this time should be constant checks to the right and towards the exit you intend to take.

Having safely entered the junction, mirrors must be checked again as you near the first exit, in readiness for the left turn signal. As more time will be needed for an inexperienced driver to check mirrors and indicate while going through the roundabout, in addition to controlling the car on a path which will swing both ways, it is important not to enter at too high a speed. When going ahead, even when no other traffic is present, instruct the pupil that they must slow down sufficiently to get into second gear. Attempting to negotiate the junction at a higher speed without a good deal of practise would probably have your pupil in a bit of a tangle at the mid-way point. Use third gear if possible however, when the pupil has gained more experience.

Turning Right at a Roundabout

Turning right (Fig. 12), as with normal road junctions, will prove more of a task for the learner and provide fun and games for the instructor. Positioning on the approach will be the first likely complication.

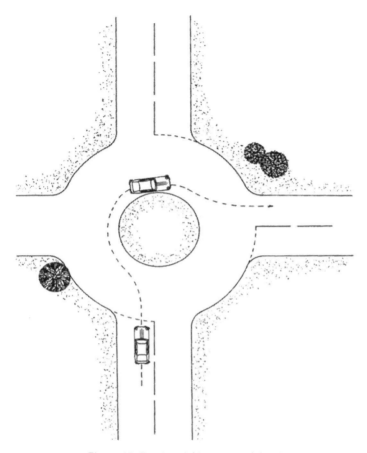

Figure 12. Turning right at a roundabout

Taking up a left of centre position is something that has already been practised and shouldn't prove difficult, but where a pupil has to be talked through a change of lanes things can become more interesting.

The move must be started well before reaching the roundabout if you are to have any chance of success. In effect, the lane change and the approach to the junction need to be treated as two separate events. A beginner has to be comfortably settled in the correct lane in good time to have full attention on what is happening when nearing the roundabout.

From the left of centre or right-hand lane position, the arrival at the give way line should be at a fairly low speed to enable the novice to enter the junction without any steering difficulties. As they head for the right-hand lane in the roundabout and begin to negotiate the central island they may have a fair bit of steering to contend with and any excess speed is asking for problems. Once more, remind the trainee that looks to the right must be accompanied by regular checks in the direction they intend to be heading when joining the flow of traffic.

Once within the right-hand lane of the roundabout, speed must be kept steady until the exit. As the driver nears the road before the one they want to leave by, mirrors must be checked before indicating left; in particular using the left door mirror before crossing the nearside lane on the way to the exit.

On larger roundabouts there is always the danger that another driver may come up on your left-hand side if the learner is a little slow. Tell your pupil in advance, that if it does happen they should be ready to slow down until the vehicle passes before they pull across to leave the roundabout, or if necessary, continue going around the island and take the exit you need next time around.

It is about this point where faults commonly occur... when the indicator signal is being changed from right to left. As the driver reaches for the lever, steering may be temporarily forgotten, or when told to signal left, they may be tempted to change lanes immediately. Either of these errors will see the car taking a rather erratic course across the final part of the roundabout. Well timed and proper instruction from you can prevent this from happening. Instruct:

"Check mirrors, hold the wheel still and signal left, look to the left and ahead then steer a smooth line to the exit."

Practising Roundabouts

Practical tuition on the move should begin where possible with left turns, then following the road ahead, and finally the more difficult right turns. This though, may be at the mercy of the layout and the location of the junctions within your area. For example, a left turn at a roundabout should be avoided if this exit leads to a busy main road. To remain in quiet surroundings it may mean having to choose the road ahead instead. You must use your local knowledge to improvise and get around this the best you can.

Most new drivers will have some teething trouble when first encountering roundabouts. Their ability to adjust speed to fit in with the flow of traffic may take a while to master and in trying hard to overcome this, observation can become a problem. They may worry about finding a suitable gap in what will probably be a greater amount of traffic than they have yet come across. And despite your instructions during the briefing, a tendency may develop for one-way observation.

This is most serious when taking the road to the right, because of the relatively sharp angle of approach to the central island. When the pupil finally remembers to look where they are going, if they happen to be heading straight for the kerb they will be left with a lot of rapid steering to do!

Steering problems of this nature also feature during left turns. The dangers here are drifting away from the line of the kerb and endangering vehicles passing on your right. Or if the novice turns blindly while staring to the right there is a risk of kerbing the nearside wheels.

Watching the pupil to ensure they are looking correctly is an obvious measure to be taken in order to prevent these faults. If the student appears to be neglecting all-round observation, remind them to look properly and if necessary instruct them to slow down more. This way, if something does go wrong, there ought to be enough time to correct the mistake before it becomes serious. On slow approaches to left turns and when you have had to stop, don't forget to include that nearside door mirror check. Most cyclists will not make allowances for a learner's lack of ability your pupil must be made to look out for them.

Directions on approach to roundabouts must be carefully worded as usual. With practise you will develop your own style of delivery but the golden rule must always be obeyed: state the destination first (roundabout), and the direction last (left). So for the first exit you would direct:

"At the roundabout I want you to turn left," and then talk the learner through the junction.

Taking the second exit from a roundabout as shown in Fig. 10 requires a little more consideration. If asked to follow the road ahead... second exit, the driver may act correctly but some will assume to continue on the road they can see directly ahead (third exit), despite the detailed briefing received earlier. Perhaps:

"Take the second road to the left," could be substituted? Again, it may work, but many will indicate left after hearing the direction. A third way is:

"At the roundabout I want you to take the second exit - treat it as a road ahead."

An instructor must still be prepared for the unexpected as no matter how clear your directions are there is no guarantee that they will be followed. You may need to experiment a little to find out what works best for your pupil, and when you do find the best way, be consistent with your directions.

For exit number three in Fig. 10, or the second exit on a standard roundabout , don't ask a novice to go 'straight on'; you may find that they do exactly that and fail to do any steering. Instead, ask them to follow 'the road ahead' and specify which exit this is. Numbering the exit roads for the pupil is certainly necessary in the early stages, but this practise can be dropped as the learner gains experience, except where you need to differentiate between two 'roads ahead' or two right turns.

We now come to the most entertaining part - attempting to make a right turn. Using Fig. 10 again as our imaginary junction we will be taking the fourth exit. What would the instruction be?

"At the roundabout I want you to turn right, leaving by the fourth exit."

Sounds okay doesn't it, but be careful! This seemingly foolproof manner of indicating your desire to turn right is how I would have delivered the direction until experience taught me a lesson; one which proved just how important accurate wording is when in the hands of a nervous driver.

Approaching a roundabout similar to the one in Fig. 10, a fine Saturday morning turned into a not so fine Saturday afternoon after I gave the above direction. I was quite impressed by the way in which my pupil entered the roundabout, he was normally a very erratic driver. Things were going along quite nicely until reaching the 12 o'clock point. He checked his mirrors and signalled left correctly, but then made a sudden lunge for what he took to be the fourth exit but what was in fact, the wrong side of the dual carriageway! Traffic was approaching in both lanes, luckily at some distance. After wrestling with the wheel I was finally forced to brake the car to a halt across both lanes. After that I modified my directions for similar roundabouts to:

"At the roundabout take the road to the right, the one after the dual carriageway."

The fifth exit from our junction is, of course, another right turn and directions can be given in a more straightforward fashion:

"At the roundabout turn right taking the fifth exit."

Even if a pupil mistook the dual carriageway for two roads in this example you would still be safe as they would end up taking the fourth road which is a right turn anyway.

Hopefully you will never experience something I have done on a few occasions during a driving lesson; having someone actually turn right into the roundabout, against the flow of traffic!

The most hair-raising example was an elderly lady who had already ploughed her way through more than 50 hours tuition and was just beginning to get the hang of it... or so I thought. She had driven well that day and wanted to be dropped off in the town centre. Towards the end of the session we had to go through the busiest roundabout in the area and I had just begun to relax as the lesson drew to an end. Then it happened; diving for the wheel I managed to swing the car around but she unfortunately stepped on the brake in panic and stalled the engine in the middle of the roundabout. The worst thing was that no one took any notice. The teeming rush-hour traffic just kept coming by on both sides as if we were a traffic island. How we got away without being hit I'll never know. When we finally got moving again and found somewhere to park clear of the junction I decided to bring the lesson to a swift conclusion and took over the wheel to drop her off.

It just goes to show that no matter how detailed the briefing and how clearly the directions are given, even with an experienced learner you must always be on guard and watch your pupil with the eyes of a hawk!

MINI ROUNDABOUTS

Signals

With mini roundabouts, as long as approach signals are given where needed, don't worry too much about giving exit signals, particularly on right turns. On some mini roundabouts the central islands are very small and this obviously requires a lot of steering; if a novice attempts to change the signal while going round there is almost always some loss of steering control. Your pupil should be encouraged to signal however, if they can do so without any loss of control.

Steering

When going ahead at mini roundabouts I have come across people who exaggerate their steering to such an extent, that the following driver thought we were going to turn left and came past on our right. There are no lanes to cut across here, so teach your pupil to keep a reasonably straight course. At some mini roundabouts there may be no need to turn the wheel at all when going ahead.

4
THE EXERCISES

A candidate may be required to carry out a number of set manoeuvres on test in order to demonstrate proper control over the vehicle, and to show that they can move away safely from a variety of situations (angle start, hill start, etc.). An exercise may also be carried out to show that the learner is able to carry out an emergency stop.

Your pupil may already have encountered slight hill starts and easy angle starts. In this chapter they are dealt with in more detail.

HILL STARTS

When to introduce hill starts as a specific exercise depends on two things: the standard of the pupil and the area in which you are teaching. Travelling any distance in some towns without meeting a hill can be very difficult while, in others, finding a gradient when you want one is the problem. Stopping on anything but a gradual incline should be avoided during a beginner's first few hours of tuition if possible, but once you are confident of a developing control and coordination from the pupil, a proper hill start may be attempted.

Preparations for moving away uphill are not radically different from a normal start. If a novice has been taught this correctly, with a few modifications the hill start should not prove to be a great hardship.

Find a safe place to stop on a hill which is on a relatively quiet area. Make sure that you do not pull up in a position likely to cause problems to other road users, for example, near the crown of the hill or on a narrow road.

Explain that what you are about to do is not much more difficult than a normal start, but several differences must be catered for.

The first consideration is engine power. Because of the slope the engine has to work harder to pull the car, so extra gas must be provided -how much more will depend on the steepness of the hill. You should advise the learner on this and guide them on the amount of gas to set as you talk the pupil through the preparations for moving off.

Secondly, to avoid the risk of rolling back, it must be made more certain that the clutch is correctly engaged. To make sure of this the driver may be told to lift the clutch pedal until a slight rise of the bonnet is seen, and once the pedals are properly set remind the learner to keep the feet still as they turn around to check the blind spot before setting off. Often, as they twist round, feet are momentarily forgotten and the pedals may be moved.

The final differences are speed and distance. Before moving away, extra time must be allowed for traffic corning up from behind as you will not be able to pull away as quickly going uphill as would be possible on a level start. To assist a safe getaway, explain the need for a firmer use of acceleration and more speed before changing up. Changing up too early on a gradient will result in a loss of momentum and the car may struggle. It will be of benefit to the pupil here to show the approximate maximum speed in each gear. A new driver may be worried at first about accelerating firmly because of the extra noise which is created; they may not be aware of how fast the car is able to be pushed in each gear ratio.

Practising Hill Starts

After the briefing, tell your pupil that you are going to practise the technique you have just described, but you are not going to drive away at first. When one hill start has been carried out you will stop again just a few yards up the hill to make another attempt.

Prepare the driver for the start. They may not recall every detail of what they have just been told so as usual, talk them through the actions. When it comes to setting the gas, guide the novice as mentioned earlier - only your judgement can tell how much power will be required for the slope you have picked. Having settled the feet; remind the pupil once more to keep them steady as they check the mirrors and the blind spot. If the feet do happen to move, start the procedure again from setting the gas. If there is no obvious gap in any oncoming traffic, don't keep the driver twisting round as this is sure to cause stress and movement of the feet. Let them watch the traffic in the rear-view mirror until a possible gap is seen, then they can look around again to check the blind spot just before setting off.

As you are not intending to drive away into the flow of traffic, you need not wait for a huge gap before making the move of a few yards further up the slope, but be sure to move only when you can do so without causing problems for other road users. When you do come to start off, a right turn signal may mislead others into thinking you are about to pull into the traffic stream, so it is best not to indicate at this point but do instruct the pupil to signal left before stopping again if there is anyone to witness your actions. A signal need not be given, though, if there is no one to see it.

While doing this exercise you must always be ready to make use of the parking brake. As the novice begins to set off there is always the possibility that there may be some roll-back. If the roll is only slight, however, don't pull the brake on in panic, simply instruct:

"Slowly bring the clutch up a little."

Only if the pupil is definitely losing control should you resort to physical action. The same applies to when the car is being brought to a halt. You must remember to give the order *"Keep your feet still,"* as soon as the vehicle stops otherwise they may inadvertently relax and naturally the release of the footbrake will mean you must quickly apply the parking brake to prevent any rolling back.

After a couple of practise starts the time comes to complete a full hill start and this means, of course, driving away to join any other traffic that may be present. If problems have been experienced, however, more attempts should be made to put things right. If moving further up the slope would put you close to the crown, swap seats and manoeuvre the car yourself so that you are in a suitable position to begin again.

Point out to the learner that now you are about to drive off from the slope, you must choose your gap more carefully - the relatively small gaps used for practising are no longer sufficient. As with any other start, you must be able to pull out into the traffic without causing any other vehicle to reduce speed or change direction. This time a signal should be considered if it will help others, but don't sit there with the indicator flashing while an endless stream of traffic passes. This gives a misleading impression and can intimidate other people, especially those on two wheels. If you do need to signal, do it just before releasing the parking brake and pulling out. And do make sure that the gaps you choose initially are fairly long so that there is no real pressure on the learner.

With practise, hill starts can be carried out on progressively steeper inclines. Where steep downhill slopes are encountered, second gear may be selected for moving off, this will give a better, smoother control than first gear.

ANGLE STARTS

It is almost certain that a pupil will have had to move off at an angle (from behind a parked car) during the first few lessons, so by the time you begin to work on this as a set exercise they should already have some idea of what to do. If not, refer to the section in chapter 2 for details of the initial briefing. You will need to recap on the basic safety rules and emphasise the importance of plenty of all round observation while moving out. If the angle is a sharp one as the car moves off it will mean the front swings out in a wider arc. In this situation, traffic which may be approaching from the front will be affected just as much, if not more than, traffic coming from behind.

In addition, instruct your pupil that once the obstruction has been cleared, a check in the mirrors before picking up speed is essential. Many drivers neglect this check as the vehicle is straightened up and are frequently taken by surprise when they are suddenly overtaken by a vehicle they never even realised was there.

Practising Angle Starts

The first real angle start should not be made too difficult, a gap of about one and a half car lengths would suffice and even this amount of space will seem small to a beginner. Prepare your pupil for moving off, and wait until the road is clear of any approaching traffic before attempting to start. Apart from the fact that other road users could be endangered if there is any loss of control it will place unwanted pressure on a new driver who has to contend with an oncoming vehicle.

Tell your student that the car must be kept under a slow clutch control while the bulk of the steering is being done. What you will have to be alert for initially is a loss of this control. As you begin to move, remind the pupil to hold their feet still and ensure that they continue to check ahead and behind as the vehicle begins to swing out. Clutch control can often slip during this exercise because the novice is so concerned about the obstruction in front, they tend to concentrate so much on steering that the feet may be forgotten and the clutch may start to rise. As speed picks up the pupil may then freeze with the steering also and give you two problems to deal with.

If the learner has been allowed to practise clutch control on numerous occasions before attempting this manoeuvre, with luck there shouldn't be too many problems. But if tension or a lack of coordination result in a loss of control, you may find yourself being propelled toward the far kerb at speed! If this happens you must react quickly to pull the wheel back and regain control over the car. The loss of control is quite common at this stage, hence the desire for a clear road before starting.

At some point during the practising of angle starts, if the driver fails to get the steering on quickly enough or travels a little too far forward, you may find yourself becoming uncomfortably close to the obstruction. If this happens, and you are in any doubt whatsoever about whether the car will be cleared, tell your charge to stop or use the parking brake if need be and explain why. It is no good continuing forward and hoping *'we just might do it'*. If you are not certain, stop and reverse to allow more room, do not take any chances! Apart from the expense of a collision it would not do the learner's confidence any good at all.

When good control over this exercise has been established the pupil may be allowed to move away when traffic is approaching, providing, of course, a safe opportunity on a wide enough road arises. Over the subsequent lessons the gap can be gradually reduced until they are able to pull out confidently from what would be a normal parking position between two cars.

This manoeuvre is required on test in order to prove that a candidate has the ability to move out safely from a confined position, something which is becoming an increasingly common necessity as parking spaces shrink.

Make it a part of your practise routine each lesson once the exercise has been introduced. It may be the first thing your pupil has to do on the big day just to drive away from the test centre. Here, while under the stress of examination nerves, control may suffer to some extent and to overcome this it pays to make sure that like all the other manoeuvres, it can be done well.

THE EMERGENCY STOP

The emergency stop is not a compulsory test exercise, but is carried out on roughly a third of tests on a random basis. As more and more cars are now fitted with some kind of anti-lock braking system, the need for this exercise is brought into question, but you should still teach this exercise to ensure that your pupil has the ability to brake firmly to a fairly quick stop should the need arise.

I have known quite a few instructors who teach this subject not as part of a lesson programme, but as a bit of an afterthought, or even on the very hour before going into the test centre. The pre-test drive and, indeed, the previous few lessons should be about getting the candidate settled down and adding the final polish, not filling a probably tense and worried mind with yet more information that will more than likely be harder to retain at this nervous time. Besides, how can the pupil be said to be ready for test if they cannot confidently perform all the manoeuvres before setting off on the day?

From the amateur instructor's point of view, however, the introduction of an emergency stop at quite an early stage of tuition is vital... you are without the luxury of a dual brake. As the novice is gradually taken into busier areas it is quite possible, of course, that a real emergency may arise. In fact, it may happen when you least expect it on a deserted side street. If this does occur and you are travelling at a reasonable speed, you have little chance of stopping the vehicle safely with the parking brake... you may not even get your hand to it in time. The beginner must, therefore, be capable of dealing with this.

Obviously, for safety, this exercise must only be practised on a fairly empty road. Find a suitable place away from the main flow of traffic and pedestrians. Having picked a stopping place, you can then go through the theory with your pupil.

There are certain points which must be picked out. To begin with you must impress on your pupil the need for a fast reaction. When the time comes for an emergency stop whether for real or in practise, there will be little time for thought. Tell them that you will make sure it is clear behind before any emergency stop and they should only be concerned with bringing the car to a halt quickly.

Although the car has to be stopped quickly, it must also be kept under control. To do this, progressive braking has to be employed, firm to begin with in this instance and then progressively harder until the vehicle stops. The initial touch on the brake is often the important part. Kicking or jumping on the pedal must be avoided... a good firm push is perhaps the best way of describing the method used. The clutch should go down as normal and both hands must be kept on the steering wheel until the car is at rest.

If your car does not have an anti-lock braking system, and the driver is unduly harsh on the brakes the likely outcome will be locked wheels and a skid. The pupil needs to be made aware of this, so that they know what is happening if this does occur. It is a good idea to discuss the causes and cures of skidding with the student at this point. It's an area of driving few learners know much about and here is an opportune moment to teach them. If the pupil is unaware of what locked wheels are, explain this first.

If you ask a beginner what the main cause of skidding is, they will usually answer with 'ice or snow', but these do not cause skids. If a vehicle was travelling in a straight line at a constant speed over a sheet of ice there is no reason why it should skid. It is only when the driver does something to change the forces acting on the car that a loss of control could occur. Braking forces the weight of the car forwards on to the front wheels, acceleration does the reverse of this, and steering throws the weight of the vehicle to left or right. It is, therefore, driver errors such as excessive braking, harsh acceleration and sudden steering movements which create skids, not the weather conditions.

The first thing to do in the event of a skid is to get the feet off the controls. Having done this, the wheels should regain their grip and if the car has drifted off course the steering can be brought back under control. If the back of the car has swung to the left, for instance, the wheel should also be turned to the left to straighten the car, but the wheel must not be turned so far that a swing is started in the opposite direction. Once steering control has been regained, the brake can be used again.

Advanced knowledge of skid control is not required for the purposes of an emergency stop. Just advise the pupil that if a skid does ever occur while doing this exercise, all they need do is to take the foot from the brake for a moment and then brake again less harshly. Although the car will travel further if this has to be done, at least when the brake is released the steering can be used to get out of trouble if necessary; if the wheels remain locked, there is no steering control whatsoever.

Practising the Emergency Stop

After the briefing, the pupil may feel apprehensive about the prospect of the first emergency stop. Calm any fears by mentioning that the first stop or two will be from quite slow speeds, perhaps about 15 - 20 mph. This allows for them to become accustomed to how the car reacts under firm braking without having to worry about speed too much. Show what signal you will give when you want the stop to be performed. Make this a clear and unique signal which could not be mistaken for anything else.

When ready, make sure the road behind is completely clear and then get the driver to set off. Instruct your pupil that you want them to change up through the gears as normal, and attempt to make normal progress.

Before signalling the stop, as well as using your mirror you should have a quick check over your shoulder to make sure nothing is in the blind spot. Ensure you are not too close to any parked cars or junctions, and also consider the presence of any pedestrians who may be startled when you brake to a sudden stop. When you are sure it is safe, give the signal, and while keeping an eye on the road watch the driver's feet as they perform the stop.

A common fault is declutching before braking. This can increase the risk of the wheels locking when the driving force is suddenly taken away from them, particularly on a loose or slippery surface. It is a fault which should be corrected. With a wet road surface, a slight skid will be hard to avoid and is not really a serious error, whereas a more pronounced slide will be a problem unless the candidate shows an ability to correct and control the skid as described earlier.

Declutching too late will result in the engine stalling. While this may not be a major fault - the main concern is that the car is stopped quickly and safely, it is best to keep the engine running so they are ready to move off again.

If the learner is slow to react or brakes too gently, then more practise is obviously needed.

Once the stop has been completed, instruct the learner to apply the parking brake in case of any gradient, and then if the exercise was successful you can move off again and try from a higher speed. If something went wrong, get the pupil to pull over into a proper parking position before discussing the mistake.

Whether you intend to drive on or park, an extra safety check should be done at this point. After an emergency stop, there is usually a gap on the nearside; this may be enough room for a cyclist to sneak through. To eliminate any chance of danger, teach your pupil to check over both shoulders before continuing after this exercise.

After the preparations have been made for setting off again, instruct the driver that you are going to move away as normal, that is a signal should be considered and a safe gap must be chosen if there is any approaching traffic. Many beginners will feel an urge to set off instantly to get out of the way of other vehicles. This can cause danger in itself if another motorist who was planning to overtake is taken by surprise. Ensure the pupil goes through the proper routine and doesn't rush, even if you are creating a temporary blockage.

Where space allows, the emergency stop can be practised until the driver is able to make a controlled stop from around 30 mph. It will increase the pupil's ability and confidence to be capable of stopping successfully from such a speed.

Once the exercise has been mastered, it need not be done on every lesson, an occasional reminder will suffice. If conditions were dry, however, when it was first attempted, it should be practised again the first time an opportunity arises in the wet. Braking technique does require more mastery on a slippery surface and a test candidate must be capable of stopping quickly under any weather conditions.

REVERSING

This can be a confusing time for the learner as not everyone finds it easy to drive a car backwards. Some can take to it fairly naturally but others may find their progress floundering to a halt. When problems are experienced with a manoeuvre, it often affects the pupil's driving standard as a whole. It should follow then that reversing is not to be attempted too early, at least not until a driver has shown reasonable mastery of the clutch and is able to exert a fair degree of control over the car while going forwards!

Initially, a beginner should only be taught to reverse in a straight line and even this can be made to look like hard work by some people. They find it awkward turning round in the seat, they get neck ache, and many individuals have a tendency to steer the car way off course when in fact, the wheel need not have been turned at all. Some inexplicable aspect of psychology seems to step in where reversing is concerned.

Even students who have previously shown good car control may not find reversing easy. While trying to orientate themselves to driving backwards they can seem to forget everything they knew about clutch control.

Start by finding a quiet, level stretch of road where you will not be too close to junctions or bends etc. Park the car and explain what you are going to do.

There are certain laws and rules to be obeyed when reversing and these should be discussed before going into the practical side of things. If the learner is putting as much into their tuition as they should be, they ought to have some knowledge of these from the Highway Code. The basic rules are:

- Ensure the way is clear behind before you begin reversing
- Keep the speed low by using clutch control
- Do not reverse when there is traffic closely approaching from behind
- Never reverse from a minor road or driveway on to a major road
- You must not reverse your vehicle for a greater distance than is really necessary, few people realise that this is an offence.

This must be borne in mind while you are practising. Apart from it being an offence to reverse for more than a reasonable distance, it can place a lot of strain on the neck of a driver who is not accustomed to twisting round for a period of time. You will need to keep the reverse going for long enough to let the pupil get the feel of it, but don't overdo it.

Having explained the basic rules, you can then move forward into the reversing position. As many beginners will turn the wheels unnecessarily or over-steer, a position close to the kerb will often result in scuffed tyres. To avoid this, have your pupil drive forward and stop parallel to the kerb but about half a metre away. Explain that this position will always be taken up in future before reversing.

A point worth mentioning here is with regard to the blind spot check before moving away. When taking up the reversing position, because the distance you need to move may only be very short, many novices tend to ignore the normal checks; they associate this with driving away. If this happens, ask your pupil to imagine they were in the position of a cycle rider; what would go through their mind if they were just about to pass a parked car and the vehicle started moving? That blind spot check is just as important here as at any other time and it must be carried out before moving even a very short distance.

Practising Straight Reversing

Having gained the starting position, the first thing to do is to tell your pupil how to select reverse gear. This can be a little awkward on some makes of car so let them try this several times before carrying on.

Next, instruct your pupil how to get ready for the manoeuvre; explain that while reversing, they need to be able to look behind comfortably without stretching the neck too much. To do this properly the driver must turn in the seat a little. Get your trainee to do this, but make sure they don't turn so far round that they will have difficulty in reaching the pedals. To facilitate easier movement, the seatbelt may be removed, though I for one discourage this as it can easily get overlooked after the manoeuvre. When a person does have problems turning because of the belt, this can often be cured simply by pulling it away from the neck and tucking it under the right arm. Sometimes, though, this may be insufficient and the seatbelt will just have to be removed.

Preparations can now be made for moving off. Once the car is in gear, get the pupil to turn round and look through the rear window. Ask them to pick out an object some distance behind which appears to be in a straight line with the car - another parked vehicle would be ideal. They can then use this as a guide while reversing and it should help them keep in a straight line. Now set the gas and have the clutch brought to bite as normal.

Another check for you is to watch the driver's grip on the wheel. The right hand should be near the top and the left hand somewhere between the 'half-past' and 'quarter-to' positions. What you are looking out for especially though is a relaxed grip. If a beginner is holding the wheel too tightly they are certain to pull the wheel to the left as they twist round in the seat. Encourage a gentle grip. The lighter it is, the more likely the car will keep itself on a straight course with no interference from the driver.

Just before moving, instruct the driver to make a final check to the front and over the right-hand shoulder for approaching traffic or pedestrians who may cross behind your car. Pedestrians and cyclists will frequently come from the blind area to the right and quite obliviously venture behind the vehicle, even when it is moving.

With everything in place you may then reverse for a short distance – about two or three car lengths should be far enough. If any steering needs to be done, avoid using the words left and right. When a driver has turned in the seat their left and right are effectively switched round and they will easily get confused. To get around this, instruct the learner to turn the wheel towards or away from the kerb, which is much simpler.

Steering in reverse gear poses problems for many learner drivers. Using the instructions towards or away from the kerb will work with some people, but everyone responds differently. Imagine yourself as a new driver; you are in the process of doing a straight reverse but the car has begun to drift away from the kerb. You have been told to turn towards the kerb and as you look through the rear window the kerb is to your right. You want the car to go in that direction so you turn to the right, what happens? The car drifts even further away! This is the dilemma facing many newcomers to reversing and even though you may avoid using the directions of left and right, the driver may still have these fixed in their mind.

It is important to keep the speed very slow during this exercise, if the novice cannot control the speed they have little chance of reversing properly. The solution to this, though, should be fairly easy. You have already given a lesson in clutch control before teaching junctions, so give this lesson again allowing your student to drive forward while doing so. Then inform them that clutch control works exactly the same when going backwards and return to reversing.

If you are lucky enough the reverse may go well first time, but usually several attempts have to be made before being successful. If this is true of your pupil, each time control is definitely slipping away, stop the reverse and return to the starting position. Driving forward again gives the learner a short break and makes sure you don't run out of space for reversing.

Where real difficulties arise, it may be a good idea to leave the exercise temporarily and practise normal driving for a while before returning for a further attempt. Apart from giving the driver breathing space, it will save wear and tear on the car. Extended use of clutch control can build up a lot of heat within the plates which results in rapid wear. Normal driving will give the clutch time to cool down.

A straight reverse is one of the exercises candidates may be asked to do on a driving test, but it will be on the right hand side of the road (don't ask me why!). So in future lessons, you should practise pulling over to the right hand kerb and reverse for a couple of car lengths, before driving off and back into a normal driving position.

Practise the straight reverse until the pupil can maintain a parallel line and a steady speed throughout. When they can do this they are ready for the next manoeuvre, which many find the most difficult of all... the left-hand reverse.

Left Hand Reverse

Reversing around a corner was dropped as a test exercise in 2017. Is it still an essential skill however and should be taught to any new driver.

Reversing around a corner can often be quite a challenge for many drivers. The purpose of this exercise is to show a driver's ability to control the car in reverse while exercising proper observation around the vehicle. The reverse does not have to be carried out with pin-point accuracy and there is no set distance from the kerb which has to be maintained, as long as the line taken is fairly constant and not excessively wide.

How much the learner can get away with will depend on the width of the road; on a narrow road more accuracy is called for. Basically, while reversing around the corner, the driver should avoid touching the kerb and the car must not be allowed to drift so wide that it may endanger or obstruct other drivers entering the road.

Reversing Practise

Choose a quiet area with a suitable junctions (avoid crossroads), and instruct the pupil to pull up just before the road you are going to reverse into. The corner should not be sharp but a gentle sweeping curve. For the first one or two reverses it is best to go through the manoeuvre in four stages (Fig. 13).

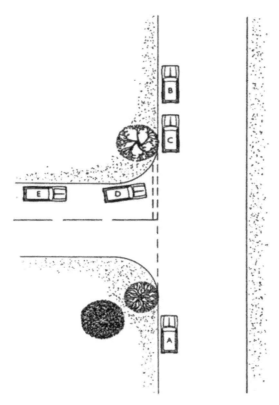

Figure 13. Left hand reverse.
A-B stage 1; B-C stage 2; C-D stage 3; D-E stage 4

Using the diagram to emphasise your directions, explain that the first stage is simply to drive past the junction and stop in the reversing position as described for the straight reverse. The car should be stopped just far enough past the junction to be able to see the full sweep of the curve through the rear window. Also, teach your pupil that as they pass the road, they must look down it to make sure it is clear to back into as well as checking mirrors. You will need about three or four car lengths in which to straighten up after the corner. If there is not much room for this, find another road.

If a signal is required before stopping, make sure that it is properly timed... too early and others may think you are turning into the road, but too late and a following driver may not have time to react.

Having moved forward and taken up the reversing position, stage two can begin. Inform the pupil that the second stage is just a straight reverse which has already practised, and get them ready to move off. This time though, tell the driver that you want them to stop in a specific place near the corner, and you will let him know when this point is reached. This will be the turning point; looking through the kerbside rear window you should be able to judge where this is for your vehicle. When it is clear, start the movement, and when you near the turning point give the signal to stop and instruct your learner to secure the car; that is to apply the parking brake and select neutral. Then move on to stage three.

Now is the time to stress the importance of correct observation. Instruct your pupil that at this point of the reverse, a check to the front of the car must be made before continuing. As they begin the turn, the front of the car will swing out and could endanger oncoming vehicles. If something is approaching which is close enough to be affected, you must stop and wait for a safe opportunity to continue, although the reverse could be kept going where the road is obviously wide enough to allow oncoming traffic free passage.

Tell your driver now to look through the rear window at the kerb line they are attempting to follow. Get them to mentally mark its position; perhaps they can find a part of the car's fittings or a mark on the window which appears to be sitting on the kerb edge. This is the new reference point; ask them to remember it for future reference. To keep this reverse accurate, the pupil will need to steer just enough to keep the kerb in view in its present position. Make them understand this and explain that if the kerb disappears from view, they will have to turn a little towards the kerb. If more of the kerb comes into view, this means they are becoming closer and the wheel will have to be turned away from the kerb to correct this. Let them know that once the car is roughly on the correct course, any steering movements required to adjust the position are likely to be quite small, otherwise you will find them turning far more than is necessary and making hard work of what could have been a much simpler task.

Before moving again, you must make another comment about safe observation, which is more important than the accuracy of the reverse. Although you want them to follow the line of the kerb, tell the pupil that they mustn't just stare at it all the while. They must also glance regularly through the rear window for signs of approaching traffic or pedestrians crossing the road.

Instruct them now to check all round the car again and if it is clear, to release the parking brake and carry on.

As the car is going through the corner, resist the temptation to stare at the kerb yourself as your main consideration is to keep a look out for other road users. As always, you must also keep an eye on the pupil. If the vehicle drifts off course, instruct them on which way to steer to correct it, but if control is obviously being lost, stop and return to the starting position to try again. Ideally, the driver should aim to keep the car at the same distance from the kerb all the way through the reverse, but don't worry if there is a little wandering as accuracy does not have to be absolutely perfect.

About half-way through the corner, get the driver to stop for a moment to make a check over the right-hand shoulder. There is a point when this area becomes a potentially dangerous blind spot and a look round to cover it is essential. If something is approaching which could be affected, again you must wait for it to pass. Carry on if or when it is safe until reaching the point where the wheels need to be straightened, then instruct the pupil to stop and apply the parking brake. This time they may remain in gear as the halt will only be momentary. In future, when making the check to the right halfway through the corner, it is not necessary to make a definite stop unless it is to wait for someone. A quick look round can be carried out while on the move.

Stage four is to straighten up the wheels and then to continue reversing in a straight line for some distance; far enough back to demonstrate an ability to keep a straight line and to leave the junction clear. This part is where many beginners start to go wrong; over-steering or turning at the wrong time (whether it be too late or too early) are very common faults and, with some individuals, can take an awful lot of practise to put right.

The pupil will probably be aware of what needs to be done to finish off the manoeuvre, but may not know how much to turn the wheel or even which way to steer! You must guide them on this and before making any further movement, stress the importance of lengthening observation now. Rather than using the kerb as a reference, they must now look straight down the road into which they are reversing. If another car is parked behind, this can be used as a guide to help the learner judge when their own vehicle is parallel. They must not be allowed to stare at the steering wheel while straightening up. Many will do this in the mistaken belief that it will tell them when the wheels are in line - this is a sure way to disaster. The only way to straighten up safely and successfully is to look where the car is going, through the rear window!

The manoeuvre can now be completed. If anything went wrong, give an explanation of how to correct the error and then go through the four-stage reverse again. If the first attempt went well, you may allow the driver to try the exercise without all the mid-stage halts unless, of course, road users approach, when stopping will have to be considered.

One problem frequently encountered while reversing is traffic coming along the road you are entering. If this occurs, instruct your student to stop and apply the parking brake. Often, drivers will then pull around you to continue on their way, but you must be prepared to move forward and clear the junction, especially if the road is narrow or visibility is restricted. In either of these cases it could be risky for the other vehicle to cross the centre-line in order to pass you. If the oncoming motorist shows any hesitation whatsoever about coming around you, get out of the way!

Many people do have problems with learning to reverse and you may find a practical demonstration will help if normal instruction appears to fail. One lady I had the pleasure of teaching experienced a great many problems with her reversing despite every piece of advice I could think of and much practise. She failed her test on two occasions due to a lack of control. I remember the story she told at a dinner party she gave and later related to me.

"On my first test," she said, *"Things were going quite nicely until the white line suddenly jumped under my wheels. I was ready next time though, on my second test I watched the line like a hawk, then bugger me if the kerb didn't leap out and hit me!"* Happily on her third attempt the reverse went well and she passed.

Once reversing has been introduced, it should be practised regularly, although if the pupil finds real problems with the manoeuvre and this begins to affect their driving as a whole, leave it for the time being and reintroduce it at a later date. On practise sessions, you should aim to achieve a greater accuracy, but always emphasise the need for safe observation; regard for other road users is always paramount.

While all this practise is going on, as well as giving instructions, you have several other jobs. You must keep your eyes open for other traffic and pedestrians, check the position of the car - if it becomes a potential danger do not allow the reverse to continue, and watch the pupil to ensure they are looking when and where necessary; and that they are ready to react.

TURNING IN THE ROAD

This manoeuvre, described by most as the 'three-point turn', requires the driver to co-ordinate all the controls and carry out good all round observation; not an easy task! It is a good exercise in car control but should certainly not be attempted too early. A learner must be able to reverse the car satisfactorily and be fairly competent in all aspects of normal driving before allowing them to combine all these skills in one exercise.

Select a road which is fairly wide to begin with and without an adverse camber; preferably a flat area if possible and, of course, out of the way of other traffic. Have a diagram ready (Fig. 14), or prepare to draw one to show the basic movements, and then give a description of the turn in the road. It does not have to be done in three movements, just make as few as you can.

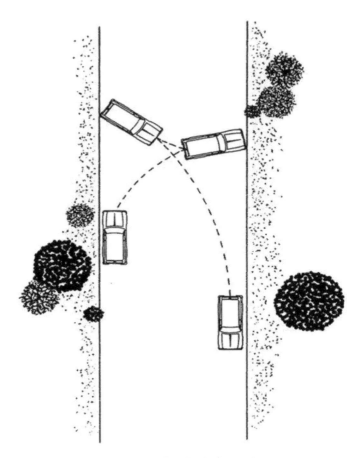

Figure 14. Turning in the road

The turn is an exercise in co-ordination, but clutch control is probably the most important part of it; if the car is kept slow enough the rest should fall into place. There is a tendency with many people, however, to turn the steering wheel slowly when the vehicle is at low speed, and when they try to turn more quickly the car mysteriously accelerates! This has to be overcome. Impress on your pupil the need for a very slow clutch control but rapid steering, the way they have controlled the vehicle when pulling out from behind parked cars. Then describe the manoeuvre.

"The basic idea is to prepare for moving off as normal. Take the usual observation checks behind and also make sure the road is clear for some distance ahead. When it's safe, you must then move very slowly forward while steering rapidly and fully to the right. Look both ways as you cross the road, and as you approach the far kerb turn quickly back to the left before stopping. We're aiming to stop about a foot from the kerb and we want to avoid hitting the kerb as this can cause tyre damage."

"Once at the kerb, the first thing you must do is apply the parking brake. Most roads have some sort of slope or camber and without the brake the car is obviously going to roll. The parking brake only takes a second to use so don't forget to apply it."

"Having applied the parking brake, you then need to change into reverse gear and bring the clutch to biting point just like you normally do when moving off. When you're ready, a check must be taken all round the car; then if it is safe you can slowly reverse, turning the wheel quickly and fully to the left. For the first half of the reverse, attention should be concentrated over the left-hand shoulder, but about half-way across, glance to the right and then turn to look over your right-hand shoulder."

"Eyes should be focused on the kerb as the car draws near, and the steering needs to be turned back to the right as much as possible before stopping the same distance of about a foot from the edge. This turning back of the wheel is very important as it sets the wheels up correctly for the next move you're going to make."

"Next, the parking brake must be set again, first gear selected, and the car prepared to move off. Checks must be made both ways, and when safe you can start forward, still slowly, but steering quickly to the right. When you are sure that the tyres are clear of the kerb you can straighten up and move into a normal parking position."

Because of the comparatively complicated movements entailed in this manoeuvre, I would recommend that after the verbal description has been given, you also swap seats and do a practical demonstration. This will help to ensure a clearer understanding of the exercise.

Having changed seats, point out how much room will be needed for the turn, ensuring there are no parked cars which could restrict your movement. Also, the manoeuvre must not be done near to a bend if the view is restricted, or in close proximity to a junction. Finally, tell your student to look out for lampposts, telegraph poles etc. near the kerb edge. If the car overhangs the pavement during the turn these may cause danger to the vehicle; avoid them.

When you demonstrate the turn, keep it slow and explain each movement as you go along. Once you have completed the reversing part, point out how close the far kerb appears to be to the front of your car. It often appears as if there is insufficient space to complete the manoeuvre. This results in many learners panicking over the last part of the exercise. If you bring it to the novice's attention here, and then demonstrate how much room there really is by finishing the move with clearance to spare, it will give them much more confidence when they are in the situation of having to make this turn themselves.

Practising the Turn

As your trainee comes to make their first effort, try to instil in them a systematic procedure. They will often try to do everything at once and end up losing control. The method should be to prepare fully for the move, then to carry out the observation, and when it is safe the move itself can be made as the third part. If the pupil attempts to do all these things at once, co-ordination is almost certain to suffer or they will forget to look. The manoeuvre must be done at a nice steady pace and should not be rushed under any circumstances. You have already described and demonstrated what to do, but as usual with a new exercise you are required to talk to the pupil through each stage of the manoeuvre.

The first part should be the easiest, but once at the far kerb new drivers will often get themselves into a fluster if other traffic approaches. Hopefully, if you have picked a quiet enough road, this situation will not happen, but if it does, keeping to a methodical procedure will help control the situation. Teach your pupil to ignore any other vehicles for the time being while they carry on with preparations for the next move. If they show signs of rushing, slow them down. Only when they are ready to move need they be concerned about tackling any other road user.

If the vehicle is still there waiting, and unfortunately they often are as they seem to think they are doing you a favour, you must diffuse the situation. To take the pressure off the pupil, providing you check to make certain the way is clear, invite the other motorist through. In future, when the learner has more or less mastered the exercise, you need not wave other drivers through. As long as the pupil is aware of where they are and what they are doing, the exercise can be completed while others wait.

When approaching motorists do stop, it is important to remember that they can move off again at any time and many novices forget this. It is absolutely essential at all stages that no matter what has happened, the learner has a final check all round just before releasing the parking brake. If someone who has stopped begins moving again, you must wait for them to pass and then look all round again before making any move.

If vehicles approach from both sides while you are in the middle of a turn, there is nothing to be done except to let them wait, even if this is the novice's first attempt. You cannot wave one driver through in case the other moves at the same time, so you will just have to keep calm and make sure the pupil does too.

Once preparations for the next move are complete, make certain that your trainee looks over both shoulders before reversing. Most people only look over their left-hand shoulder during this part of a turn; if something approaches from the right and attempts to pass behind you it will not be seen until it is too late.

The fact is, whichever manoeuvre is being carried out, the driver must always be on the lookout for other people, and must be prepared to give way to passing traffic - vehicles or pedestrians. If other people decide to stop and wait, fair enough; but no one must be forced into making an involuntary stop.

When the reverse does get under way, keep reminding the pupil to take their time, even if other people are waiting. If the learner is unduly worried about the presence of other traffic, reassure them that the other driver could have carried on if they had wished to. It was their decision to stop, so let them wait!

After completing the reverse part, the same rules apply. Get your pupil ready for the next move and tell them to ignore everything else while this is being done. When you are set to go, make the final checks both ways (instruct the pupil to make sure it is clear, or that people who have stopped are still waiting), and then finish the manoeuvre.

As you move forward on this final part, if the car seems a bit short on clearance don't risk hitting the kerb, tell the driver to stop and do a second reverse. Let them know that this is quite acceptable. This can be a difficult exercise to begin with and not all beginners will be able to do a 'three-point' turn first time. If you really get stuck during a manoeuvre, as a last resort you may have to take over the driving seat temporarily to sort things out.

After the first attempt, you should give any further instruction that may be required and then practise one or two more turns before driving away. If the pupil shows a complete lack of control after several turns, take a break and do some normal driving for a while.

Practise this regularly in future and after each turn, where discussion is needed, stop to do this. Otherwise you should encourage the pupil to continue driving as soon as the manoeuvre is complete.

As the pupil's skill increases, you can choose roads which become progressively narrower and more steeply cambered. Where an individual has difficulty coping with the camber during these exercises, more clutch control practise will be needed, but this time on a slope.

CLUTCH CONTROL EXERCISE ON A GRADIENT

Take the pupil to a quiet road with a slope and prepare for a normal hill start. When preparations are complete, instruct your learner that you want them to release the parking brake in a moment without the car moving backwards or forwards. Tell them that if the vehicle does creep forwards they will have to put the clutch pedal a fraction lower. This movement may only be very small, perhaps no more than a few millimetres. If the car moves backwards at all then naturally it follows that the pupil is instructed to lift the clutch a fraction to prevent this.

Instruct them to release the parking brake and if there is any roll or creeping guide them as to which way to move the clutch and by how much. When the vehicle is held stationary, wait until it is clear behind, then tell the pupil to lower the clutch a fraction in order to let the car roll very slowly backwards for a short distance. Then instruct them to carefully raise the pedal again until the rolling stops and the car is held steady. Repeat this a few times. You must not allow your car to roll against any oncoming traffic -the road behind should be clear each time this is done. If you have already begun rolling, however, when something appears, instruct your pupil on how to stop the movement without delay. If they are capable of doing this, there should be no problem, but where the pupil has difficulty in controlling the vehicle you will have to consider applying the parking brake.

Next, try the exercise moving up the slope. From the holding position, have your student raise the clutch slightly so that the car creeps slowly up the hill. Then get them to lower the clutch pedal until the vehicle stops moving. Control is much more difficult when moving upwards. Going down the slope the novice can easily feel the bite as the clutch is brought up and the car slows, but when driving upwards this is not so evident. You will have to teach them to listen to the sound of the engine. If they lower the clutch too far when going up the hill and it passes the biting point becoming disengaged, the engine note will rise. This is a warning to the driver that the clutch must be brought back up a little otherwise the car is going to begin rolling back as soon as it loses momentum. Again, repeat the upward movement several times.

If the exercise is successful at the first attempt, prepare for a normal hill start and drive away. If more practise is required however, have a break for a few minutes and switch off the engine. The clutch has to work hard during all this time and deserves a rest. Whenever you do stop for a breather or to give an explanation which takes more than a few moments, the engine should be turned off. Leaving it running is simply a waste of fuel and not very environmentally friendly.

This exercise will increase a novice's control and confidence on gradients and an improvement should be evident during the turn in the road exercise. If no progress is seen straightaway, continued clutch control exercises will eventually take effect.

REVERSING AROUND SHARP CORNERS

Up to teaching the turn in the road, the left-hand reverse should already have reached a fairly good standard. Once some mastery of turning in the road has also been accomplished you may teach a new reversing skill - backing into a road with a right-angled corner. Unless you live in a newly built area, these sharply angled corners will be as commonplace as the sweeping variety. A learner driver needs to be taught how to reverse competently around both types.

Find a sharp corner in a side street, stop the pupil before the opening of the road, and explain the need for a different technique with this sort of angle.

To begin with, they must position a little further out from the kerb. Allow them to get too close and the tyres are sure to make contact with the kerb if they turn too early.

When the turning point is reached, the kerb will appear to be in a different position than that which was used for the sweeping reverse. Tell your student that initially, you will help them to find this turning point. At the point of turn, rather than steering to keep the kerb in view, explain that it will be necessary to steer quickly towards the kerb until the wheel is on full lock (you may to explain what full lock is). In effect, the pupil needs to imagine the rear left-hand wheel as a hinge. The car should be pivoted on this hinge when the rear wheel is in line with the apex of the corner (Fig. 15). With the pupil now aware of these facts, move past the opening and take up your position.

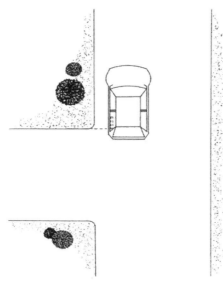

Figure 15. Turning point for sharp corners

Practising the Sharp Reverse

Instruct the driver to make ready for reversing. Start them when the way is clear, and call them to a halt when the rear wheels have become level with the corner of the kerb. Ask the pupil to note the position of the nearside kerb. Rather than being seen in the back window it will appear in one of the side windows, or may perhaps be hidden behind one of the door pillars. Remind them that this is the turning point for a sharp corner and must not be confused with a sweeping corner where the kerb should be seen in the rear window.

Return to your starting place now. Before going any further explain that when they actually begin to turn the corner, it may appear as if the car is going to run over the kerb, but this would only happen if they have turned too early or started too close to the kerb to begin with. Inform your pupil that observation must be carried out in similar fashion to the sweeping reverse, but with particular care at the point just before turning. At the point of turn the front of the vehicle will swing out very quickly and the driver must, therefore, be sure that nothing is closely approaching from any direction.

As you now go through the whole reverse, remind the pupil of what to do and ensure that they keep a low speed. With a sharp corner there is only one chance; unlike a sweeping reverse you are not able to continue making corrections all the way through. If the pupil is too late, or too early with the steering, the manoeuvre would have to be abandoned in favour of a fresh attempt.

When the car enters the side road, straightening up of the steering has to begin a little earlier than with more gently curving corners. Because the novice has more turning to do they must be given more time to do it, otherwise if it is left to the last moment to take off the full lock they will probably rush and end up over-correcting. You will have time to inform the driver of this after they have taken the final check to the right.

In future lessons, both types of reverse should be practised regularly if opportunities present themselves. Warn your trainee that when they are asked to do a reverse from now on it could be either type of corner that is chosen, and it will be up to them to decide which technique to use. The simple way of avoiding any mishaps with this is to stop before the road you want the pupil to reverse into, and ask them there and then which method is required for the corner. At a later stage, however, the student should just be left to decide on how to cope with the corner without being questioned; as soon as you are confident that they can tell the difference between a sharp or sweeping reverse at a glance.

REVERSING TO THE RIGHT

Reversing into a road on the right, like some of the other manoeuvres, is not required as part of the driving test. It's still something that we may all need to do at some time though so it is a good idea to teach it.

Backing into a road on the right is technically easier than a left hand reverse because the kerb can be seen much more easily through the side windows. The most difficult aspect of this manoeuvre however is the observation. More care needs to be taken because of the position of the vehicle, and more effort has to be put in to twist round sufficiently in order to take this observation.

This reverse is best left until a driver is nearing test standard. I have tried teaching both left and right-hand reversing from an early stage but found that it can lead to confusion for a beginner. Many have enough problems remembering which way to turn the wheel during a left-hand reverse. Introducing another reverse in the opposite direction at this time can complicate things even further. At a later stage, however, the reverse to the right should be tackled with reasonable ease.

Practising the Right Hand Reverse

Stop the pupil on the left-hand side of the road before the junction you are going to reverse into and give a brief explanation of what you want them to do. As you set off to take up your starting position, make sure you are safely past the opening before crossing to the far side (Fig. 16).

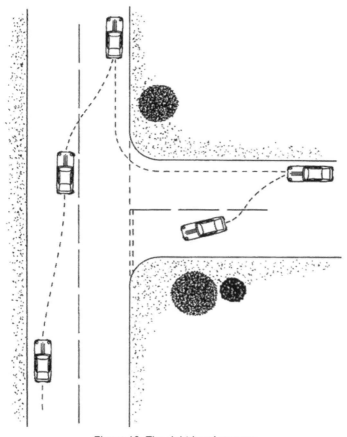

Figure 16. The right hand reverse

The first priority before beginning is a good look all round, and then instruct your pupil to look over their right-hand shoulder as the reverse is begun. When the turning point is reached, stop the car for a moment. Here the normal check to the front must be made but the pupil must also be made aware of the present situation. They are reversing on the 'wrong' side of the road and extra allowances must be catered for.

As the turn is begun, any other traffic that may arrive would be prevented from entering the side road, therefore in addition to the look ahead the driver must also be aware of what is happening on the road behind, even if this means twisting round to glance over the left-hand shoulder. If another vehicle does wish to turn right into your road you must give way and this may mean having to pull forward. Traffic coming from the front must be allowed to pass before turning is begun. The same consideration as shown on the left-hand reverse should be shown here, but where a vehicle coming from ahead wishes to turn into the same road you are reversing along, it may be easier for you and them if you carry on, unless the other driver intends to go around you.

About halfway round, a check to the left must be made for any incoming traffic. As this involves quite an amount of body movement the pupil may again find it easier to pause when doing this although some may manage it without halting. If safe, carry on up to and past the point of straightening. On this reverse you must continue for a greater distance than would be necessary for a left-hand corner. This gives room to regain your own half of the road when moving off after the manoeuvre without being too close to the mouth of the junction.

A final point about preparing to move off after the reverse has been completed. Your pupil will have to change a habit to which they have by now become accustomed; they will have to look over the left-hand shoulder rather than the right and, of course, if a signal is required this will also be to the left; seemingly obvious perhaps, but not always so to the learner. Some will still look to the right and even signal in that direction unless told otherwise!

PARKING

When starting the subject of parking with your student, whether it is into a driveway, alongside the kerb, or any other place, the first thing to stress is the importance of reversing *into* a confined space and not out of it. In reverse, the car is more manoeuvrable, making it easier to get into a limited area; and it is ALWAYS safer.

Reversing Into a Bay

In a busy supermarket area if you reverse out of a bay from between other cars, you are almost certain to inconvenience or even endanger others as you struggle to manoeuvre out of this limited space with restricted vision on both sides. If the car is reversed *into* the gap however, the driver can then clearly see what is around when setting off again, and can drive straight out from the space and be on their way with ease without causing other motorists and pedestrians to stop and wait.

Despite this, the majority of people still drive forwards into a bay. There is of course, the argument that when going shopping, this enables the boot to be reached more easily; but many do it simply because they have problems reversing.

The DVSA decided in December 2017 to include reversing out of a bay as a set exercise, therefore you will need to teach this as well, but wherever possible I would still always recommend to teach reversing in and would suggest that this is the method you should impress on your pupil as the safest option.

Reverse Bay Parking Practise

Getting into a space such as will be found in a multi-storey car park or superstore requires a similar technique to the left or right-hand reverse. Take your trainee to a suitably quiet car park, or let them practise using your own driveway or garage if you have one.

The pupil should have a sound knowledge by this stage of how to reverse the car, but will need to be shown how to set the car up for this type of parking manoeuvre. Rather than just driving past the gap and stopping at right angles with the other cars (Fig. 17a); as they pass the gap they should steer to the left and then steer quickly to the right just before stopping - or vice versa if the gap is approached from the opposite direction. They are then left with a relatively easy task of doing what is practically a straight reverse (Fig. 17b).

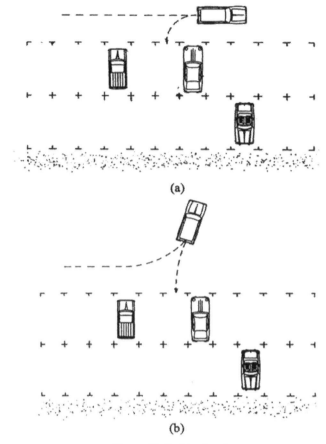

Figure 17. Parking in a bay

Safe observation is, as ever, the most important factor to impress on your pupil when practising this exercise. When you drive into a car park, others will naturally be expecting you to stop at some point to drive into a bay, but you must make sure that your driver knows what is behind them, and that before they stop or change direction to get into position they give a signal if necessary, and be aware of where other people are.

Once they begin to reverse, it is acceptable for the learner to glance in both door mirrors to help line the car up with the bay markings, but all round observation should be kept up at all times and they should be ready to stop if necessary should anyone show an intention to come past.

Reversing Out of a Bay

Driving forwards into a bay should be pretty straightforward. If the bays are in double rows as they are shown in Fig. 17, it is advisable to avoid those where you will be limited for space. If there are cars on either side or in front of you, the learner will find it much more difficult to get in and out of the bay; and you do not have dual controls to stop them should they over-run or swing the bonnet too sharply.

Make sure that they understand it will be easier if they approach from a wide position to lessen the amount of steering involved. This may involve moving away from the bay on the approach to make the necessary room, so make sure your driver is fully aware of what is behind and around them as they approach the chosen bay, and position early to avoid suddenly swinging out.

Once within the bay, reversing out should again be easy. If you do have a car alongside you, then you may have to reverse out in a straight line until you are clear of it; but when there is clear space, then teach the learner that they can steer as soon as they begin to reverse, it does not matter at this point if the front of the car swings over the white lines. Whichever way you back out, brief the pupil beforehand so that they understand what to do before setting off. You should also point out that they can reverse in either direction unless there is a one-way system operating in the car park.

Once again, safe observation is paramount. You are much more likely to get in other people's way reversing out of the bay than you would when reversing in, so all round checks need to be made continuously and courtesy shown to those around you.

Parallel Parking

The more difficult type of parking manoeuvre, where the driver has to reverse into a space between two vehicles along the kerbside... parallel parking, will no doubt give most learners much more of a challenge. In fact, many experienced motorists would rather park in the next street than attempt this exercise!

When carrying out the parking exercise on test, the examiner would not normally ask the candidate to manoeuvre into a space between two cars, but would only use one vehicle, and ask the driver to complete the exercise within about two car lengths. You may use this method if you wish to get the learner accustomed to the idea of parallel parking, but I think it is best to progress on to using a space between other vehicles at some stage to give more realistic experience and practise.

While practising this manoeuvre, do be careful not to continually use the same cars. Some owners are a little sensitive about this and have been known to come out and complain. There are some who complain that the exercise is done at all with a learner driver, but surely it is better to let them practise under the safety of supervision, than to let them pass the test without this skill then expect him to do it safely on their own?

You will need to look for a fairly large space to begin with, perhaps about two and a half times the length of your vehicle, on a quiet side street where the road is preferably flat. Instruct the pupil to pull up somewhere well before this gap. Explain that you are going to drive past the space, and will stop about halfway past and parallel to the car you intend to use. Then you will reverse into the gap in order to park parallel to the kerb. Inform the driver of what will need to be done before moving to the starting position. Use the diagram (Fig. 18), as you explain how to reverse into the space.

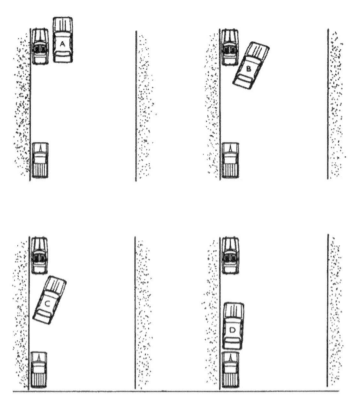

Figure 18. At position 'A', turn the wheels sharply to the left. At 'B', they should be straightened and kept like this until the rear of the car nears the kerb. At 'C' the wheels should be turned quickly to to the right. As the front swings in at position 'D', the wheels should again be straightened as much as possible before pulling forward to finish.

Instructions:

"Having stopped about halfway past the leading car, get ready to reverse and then make your usual check all round. When it's clear, go back very slowly until the rear of our car appears to be almost level with the back of the other vehicle. Make sure at this point that it is clear to the front and behind

because when you begin to steer, the front of the car will swing out like it does on a sharp reverse. If anything is approaching, wait if necessary for it to pass. Providing it is safe you will need to steer quickly towards the kerb, again like you did for the sharp reverse. Exactly how much steering you will need depends on the size of the gap and the vehicle you are trying to get behind - in most cases it will be full left lock."

"Leave the steering on left lock until you appear to be about halfway past the corner of the other car, and then quickly straighten up the wheels. Let the straight reverse continue, still very slowly, until your rear wheel is quite close to the kerb, and also keep an eye on the vehicle behind while you are doing this. When the rear wheel is close to the kerb, check the front again to make sure you're clear of the car in front and then steer sharply away from the kerb to swing the bonnet into the gap."

"Finally, when the front wheel comes near to the kerb, begin to straighten up again. You may not be perfectly centred in the space at this point so you will have to shuffle back and forth a bit to get things right. When you are in between two cars like this, always apply the parking brake before changing gears, so that if your foot slips off the clutch or you roll, there will be no danger of bumping the other vehicles."

Parallel Parking Practise

For the first attempt at parking, it is best to get the driver to stop for a moment at each of the points you have picked out.

This gives them an opportunity to check the position of the car, but more importantly it will ensure that they keep things under control at a low speed. This is especially important where the road is cambered as once the back of the car is turned into the gap it will start to run downhill. Halting at several places during the manoeuvre will prevent this becoming a problem. Forewarn your pupil that the car may begin to roll back at some point and that they will need to keep gently touching the footbrake if this happens in order to control the speed.

If the exercise begins to go wrong at some stage, don't let the trainee struggle on with it; do the sensible thing and pull out of the gap to start afresh.

Once the parking has been successfully completed, try again, but this time tell your pupil that you want them to finish as close as they can to the car in front without the need for shuffling forward in the gap. If they can do this, your driver should be informed, then they will be capable of parking in much smaller spaces than the one you are using.

Parking needs to be practised regularly, and having grasped a reasonable degree of competence at the exercise the spaces you choose can become progressively smaller, but the minimum should be a gap of about one and a half times the length of your own car.

5
DEALING WITH TRAFFIC

During a learner driver's programme of lessons, it is vital that they are not rushed into things for which they are not ready. This is a common mistake among inexperienced instructors. Many times have I witnessed a learner car dawdling along well below speed limits creating the kind of hold-up that a milk float driver would be proud of! If the novice cannot maintain a reasonable progress then they should not be out in traffic. Pushing a learner too much and leading them into situations which cause them to panic can make your job much harder, creates unnecessary hindrance or danger to other road users, and from the pupil's point of view can lead to shattered confidence which will take a long time to put right. The learning process has to be a gradual one, moving on only when you and the pupil feel ready to tackle something new.

Throughout the beginner's first series of lessons when the basics of car control and manoeuvring are being taught, you obviously cannot keep away from traffic totally. However, heavy traffic, busy junctions or complicated layouts and fast flowing roads must be avoided.

It may be necessary to drive the pupil away from home for the initial lessons if you live in a busy area or on a main road. You can then teach in a quieter place and at the end of the lesson swap seats and drive back. Once a novice has shown some progress, this could be modified; drive to a quiet starting place but perhaps allow the student to drive back if they seem capable enough. When they show signs of settling into their driving more quickly you can let them drive from the outset.

When to move on to each stage depends on several factors: the driver's ability, the type of area you are in and how busy the roads are when the lesson starts and finishes. A beginner might well be capable of driving from home on the second lesson if conditions are favourable, but if the session finishes during rush-hour traffic you would have to take over on the way back. Your own judgement has to be exercised in deciding when the individual is ready to cope with the situations that may develop during an hour or two out on the road.

Always remember just how individual people are. If you have already taught someone to drive who turned out to be a model pupil, don't expect another person to be as easy to teach. Try not to hold back when the trainee is ready for progress and not to force along where more practise is needed on subjects already covered. Everyone who learns to drive does so at their own pace. We all have different strengths and weaknesses and the skill lies in being able to bring a pupil to test standard and above without putting undue pressure on yourself or the learner.

On the first few lessons you are unlikely to cover a great distance with a newcomer to driving. But as you begin to venture out into a little traffic, even over just a few miles you might possibly have to contend with various hazards such as traffic lights, crossroads, and pedestrian crossings and so on.

Each hazard must be dealt with in turn, even if it means stopping in order to explain what has to be done.

Some people will have a fair idea of what to do at pedestrian crossings and lights while others will not have a clue. There is another type of learner who can recite the Highway Code parrot fashion, but ask them to put it into practise and they will struggle.

Many routine obstacles such as parked cars and cyclists which are met time and again can be handled while on the move, by giving the driver advice and instruction in good time on how to deal with these. Out on the road you are the driver's eyes and brain and they will often do little without your prompting. Always look as far ahead as you can to warn a beginner of even the slightest hazard; they can be very slow to react and must be given time to prepare. A parked car is simple enough to pass for most drivers, but learners on the whole tend to think no further ahead than their own bonnet and need to be given a running commentary on the changing pattern of things around them. When any potential danger is spotted, the driver must be given advice on how to prepare for and deal with it well before the time to act arises.

A parked car on the road ahead is an obvious obstruction, but don't assume the beginner has seen it, nor assume that if they have noticed it that they will take the correct action. Road sense is not an inbuilt ability, it has to be taught. In some instances people can be totally unaware of what is happening around them when they are concentrating on controlling their own vehicle. This is the main reason for not taking a novice into busy traffic at an early stage. They must first develop control over the car and be able to carry out gear changes and other actions without too much effort. Only then can you expect a pupil to start taking in their surroundings and putting some thought into what they are doing.

Giving a running commentary will help prepare your pupil for what lies ahead and will also start to develop their own sense of anticipation. It will encourage them to look and plan further ahead as they search out the hazards you have picked out for attention, and with practise they will begin to respond to dangers before they have been pointed out. That is the time to begin reducing the amount of instruction they are given.

It is during these early excursions into traffic that your work is probably at its hardest. Not only must you keep talking to your pupil and constantly watching what they are doing with hands, feet and eyes, you also have to check the dashboard occasionally as you normally would when driving yourself, be continuously planning where you intend to go next and how to get there safely and, of course, the all-important factor of other road users and what they are doing. Taking all this in can be very tiring, both for you and the learner. The strain will be similar to that experienced during motorway driving if you are doing the job properly and concentrating fully, but it does get easier with practise.

If the driver is to learn how to get about in traffic safely, one of the most important aspects of tuition is use of the mirrors. When teaching the use of these you must be thorough. Ensure they are used regularly and that the pupil takes notice of what is seen in them, especially before changing direction when others are most likely to be affected. Tell the driver well in advance that a change in direction may have to be made, and if this is necessary, the decision when to move out has to be yours until the novice gains experience. Let them know what you see and explain why you are making these decisions. This will teach them to make effective use of their own mirrors rather than just looking for the sake of it.

Many test candidates fail for not making effective use of mirrors before changing direction and can then be heard complaining:

"I was using my mirrors, the examiner just never saw me!"

To quote from a little pamphlet which used to be issued with provisional licences on the subject of mirrors; *"Just looking is not enough, you must look soon enough, judge what may happen and act accordingly."* One of my favourite quotes!

This is where many people go wrong, assuming that as long as they look in the mirrors, the job has been done. That's why the question of when and when not to move must be answered by you in the early lessons. A novice may use the mirrors when told and see the vehicle behind but without plenty of practise they will often fail to judge what the following driver is doing or about to do. They may have difficulty judging speed and distance. Despite another vehicle gaining and obviously about to pass, many would quite happily pull out anyway forcing the following driver to brake and fall back. This is not making effective use of mirrors and is something which must be indelibly imprinted in the mind of your learner.

This type of problem will be much more evident on roads with two or more lanes, where changes of directions are likely to be more frequent. Roads such as these do need to be tackled with a little foresight. The driver should be briefed on how to act and what to look out for on two-lane carriageways before being let loose on the public.

This is what you must do when approaching anything that is new to the beginner, unless you are sure the pupil is competent enough to cope with the situation without stopping for an explanation. This should be true for most minor hazards. But anything out of the ordinary, or if the driver doesn't seem to possess a great deal of road sense, your best plan is to stop even if only for a few moments to inform the learner of what to do when reaching the hazard. Stopping will ensure the pupil's undivided attention and this way the tuition given is much more likely to be understood and remembered.

While on the move in traffic, you and your pupil have much more to think about and many decisions have to be made. Relatively simple things such as when to change gear should by now be almost totally in the hands of the learner, but decisions which may affect other people are your responsibility. Your anticipation must be infinitely better than that of the average motorist. Not only must you judge what is about to happen around you but you must also be aware of the pupil's likely reactions to this, which can sometimes be thoughtless or panic ridden. So for the sake of safety a good instructor must always be thinking well ahead of the pupil.

Once you have decided on a course of action, there must be time for the instructions to be delivered and allowances have to be made for the novice's reactions, which may not always be spontaneous. By far the best aid to both of you here is in keeping well back from the vehicle in front; you not only increase the view of the road ahead, but gain vital seconds in which to act. A lot of learners try to keep in touch with the car ahead; in the back of their minds they think that if they fail to move off as soon as the person in front does they will be holding up drivers behind. You must urge your pupil to keep a good distance.

Staying well back is even more important when having to travel in the right-hand lane of a two-lane carriageway. Frequently, vehicles ahead will slow down or stop in order to turn right and there may be a gap in the parked cars on the left into which you could move for overtaking on the inside, but what must be done first? Mirror checks and judging what is happening behind and to the side, and if the space is not a large one you may need to brake and change down before switching lanes. All this takes mere seconds to an experienced motorist, but a learner who encounters this for the first time will often get only as far as checking the mirrors before having to take sudden action. If the novice had been able to start preparations from further back, they might well have stood more chance of being ready to overtake safely, or better still, if it took a few seconds longer to reach the obstruction it may well have gone by the time you arrived and the lane change would be unnecessary.

When you do have to use the right-hand lane in this kind of situation, it is good practise to instruct the pupil to check the left-hand door mirror frequently informing them that this is in case you have to move back in at any time. Warn them, in particular, to look out for mopeds which tend to weave in and out of the gaps between parked cars and in slower moving traffic the same can be said of cyclists.

It is in slow moving traffic when use of the door mirrors becomes vitally important. This is when those two-wheelers may pass on either side and then suddenly pull out in front of you to pass an obstruction or turn right.

In traffic, always be ready to take control of the vehicle if the pupil commits a serious error. This could mean giving a firm hand with the steering to prevent the driver from suddenly swerving or to correct the position of the car when it is drifting off course. The parking brake may also have to be used to pull up in an emergency. When verbal instruction fails you must take physical action quickly. If a major fault is committed by the driver, the rule is to keep calm and find a convenient place to stop as soon as an opportunity arises. You can then discuss the error and explain how to correct the mistake which was made. Halting also gives the pupil time to settle down again before returning to traffic. If possible, you should then approach the same situation again so that the learner is able to negotiate the hazard correctly in order to regain lost confidence.

TRAFFIC LIGHTS

The function and necessity of traffic lights is common knowledge to all types of road user, even someone who has never before taken to the driving seat will have a basic understanding of what the signals mean. But you are wrong to assume that everyone has a proper understanding of each phase of the traffic light sequence. Sure enough, most of the population will recognise the red light, and the same number of people will believe that the green signal means go. It does not!

Does the learner think to look before moving on as they would at any other junction? Probably not. Will they wait at the green light when the other side of the crossroads is blocked by queuing traffic? Unlikely... indeed many people tend to think that when the green light is showing that they have a right of way and will set off regardless; this is not a safe way of thinking. The rule is, of course, go, but *only* if the way is clear. Ensure your pupil knows this.

Perhaps though the most misunderstood or ignored signal is the amber light showing alone. Ask your student what this means and the likely reply will be: *'Get ready to stop'* or: *'The lights are about to change to red'*. Any good and lawful driver knows that the basic meaning of this signal is stop, but for safety the law allows some leeway. If you are already crossing the line or to pull up sharply might cause an accident you may continue. Many drivers exploit this by putting their foot down to 'beat the lights'. Because of these practises, learner drivers can easily get the wrong impression.

The novice must know what each light signal really means. They should be questioned on the subject and any lack of knowledge or misunderstanding can be cleared up by referring to the Highway Code or the Driving manual, both of which give clear explanations of the traffic light rules.

When approaching lights on red, your thought should be; 'will they change as we get closer? ' With this in mind prepare the pupil. If they are at an early stage of car control it is good policy to instruct them to change down through the gears as the speed drops so in the event of the lights changing to green, they are already in the correct gear to carry on. As the learner progresses, this can be modified, with some experience under these conditions the pupil can be taught to avoid changing down unless the lights actually change. They can then go from fourth into, perhaps, second gear; it's an easier way of driving.

When the lights are on green as you draw near you must again get ready for possible change. A mirror check is your first priority to assess how close any following vehicle is (ensure the pupil does the same). If something is quite close you will need to reduce speed to avoid the need for heavy braking in case of the amber/red light coming on. Over the final few yards, a safe way of approaching is to instruct your charge to cover the brake for a few moments so that the car slows down naturally and the driver is instantly ready to brake if need be. Once reaching the point where you would be too close to stop even if the lights did change, make sure the pupil looks for a clear passage through then tell them to accelerate again.

A check all round is essential before continuing. It may be clear 99% of the time but drivers do go through on red, particularly just after the lights have changed. Cyclists frequently ignore traffic signals completely. An emergency vehicle could be coming through or the other set of lights could have failed. Another danger is in very bright sunshine; sometimes it is almost impossible to make out which signal is showing when they are directly in the sun's rays. Always insist on your pupil taking proper observation before crossing any junction even if they have a green light.

If traffic lights do change from green to amber or red as you draw near and you have time to stop, be ready to take emergency action yourself if necessary. All drivers have to brake firmly at the lights occasionally but this is an action an inexperienced learner may be afraid to do in traffic, or they may just be slow to react. In either case you must act quickly yourself or risk crossing the line on red.

When stopped at lights, or any other obvious hold-up, teach your student to apply the parking brake before they release the footbrake or change gear, even in the very early lessons. Some instructors neglect this and in doing so lay the foundations of a potentially dangerous habit. A new driver often fails to recognise slight gradients; any roll-back is obviously hazardous and may induce panic in a nervous pupil. Also, while waiting, an absent-minded beginner may be prone to removing the foot from the clutch with the car still in gear. This is a common enough fault which will only end up with a stalled engine if the parking brake is secure. If not, the sudden jerk forward could be disastrous.

On the same lines, the selection of neutral should gradually be introduced into the driving plan. At an early stage, only use neutral when you are fairly well back in the traffic queue, or when there is a lengthy period of waiting, such as at level crossings.

While waiting at traffic lights, teach the learner not only to watch their own signals but also to keep an eye on the opposing set of lights. This way they can relax more if they can see the other lights changing and work out when the sequence will turn in their favour. When they can do this they will be able to get into gear and be ready before the cars ahead of you start moving off. Where the other lights are not visible use your own judgement in telling the driver when to get ready, and do this in good time. Leave it late and the pupil will be forced to rush and may end up stalling.

With more experience, a trainee should be encouraged to make use of neutral more often, even at the front of the traffic queue. Having been taught to read and anticipate light changes, they should be able to cope with this easily when nearing test standard. Using neutral is another thing that many instructors don't teach. I believe it should be taught for two very good reasons: it gives the driver a chance to relax tense muscles and removes the risk of that foot suddenly being taken from the clutch and, secondly, if the car is left in gear, even though the clutch is depressed it causes unnecessary wear to the bearings. Selecting neutral will help prolong the life of the clutch in the long run.

A final word about waiting at traffic lights; this is a time when traffic will naturally build up, and slower moving vehicles which may have been passed will catch up. Cyclists and mopeds may pull up very closely on either side. These must obviously be catered for; it is when they first set off from rest that they are most likely to wobble. On occasions in this situation it will be wise to instruct your pupil to hold back for a few seconds when the lights change to give time for the two-wheelers to stabilise.

PEDESTRIAN CROSSINGS

Pedestrian crossings are a hazard which every road user should understand, but guidance will no doubt improve on the novice driver's reaction to them. When a crossing is spotted ahead, give an order to check mirrors and reduce speed, in the case of a zebra crossing instruct the driver that you want them to stop if people are waiting or already stepping out. Beginners in traffic will often be reluctant to pull up unless told to do so as driving at a steady speed with no interruptions is obviously easier than stopping and starting.

Pelican crossings are a different matter. The pupil should be taught to check both sides for people as they would at a zebra, and if someone is waiting, a reduction in speed will be necessary. When pedestrians are there, the wait button has almost certainly been pressed and the lights could change at any moment.

With a change of the lights anticipated, the approach can be treated in similar fashion to normal traffic-lights, by covering the brake for a moment on the final run-up. When you have to stop, ensure the parking brake is applied while people are crossing. This is one place you don't want the car to jerk forward if the pupil makes a mistake with that clutch!

When the flashing amber light signal shows, some beginners will sit there until the crossing is absolutely deserted or may even wait for the green light, so be ready to urge them on as soon as your way is clear.

DUAL CARRIAGEWAYS

Driving along dual carriageway roads makes motoring easier in many respects, but a newcomer can have difficulty in judging where to position the car and when to change lanes. Theoretical tuition in advance is much better than just wandering on to such a road and expecting a pupil to know what to do. A novice who unknowingly dawdles along the right hand lane when the left is clear is going to cause a lot of problems.

Your best plan is to park just before or as soon as you join the carriageway and show the pupil how to make use of the lanes.

The first rule is keep to the left if it is clear. If one or two obstructions have to be passed, all that needs to be done is to check the mirrors, indicate if necessary, move out far enough to give the obstruction adequate clearance and return to the left-hand lane (you do not need to signal for the obvious move back to the left).

In this situation, the white line may be straddled providing it is only for a short while. If there are regular obstructions, you must avoid constantly moving in and out as this would be difficult for the learner and confusing for other traffic. When this is the case, or if there is a long line of parked cars, move into the right-hand lane and stay there until the left becomes clear to use again.

The second likely problem for a learner is making a right turn. Whether this is at the end of the road or through an intersection, a change of lanes may have to be made. The difficulty many inexperienced drivers have is of knowing when to change lanes and judging the speed and distance of traffic behind. On urban dual carriageways traffic tends to move very quickly, often well in excess of the legal speeds. A new driver often fails to realise just how fast some of these vehicles might be gaining and will pull out regardless. On the other hand, a constant stream of overtaking traffic may be intimidating to the beginner and they may be reluctant to change lanes at all.

The first thing you must do is to get your pupil to move out soon enough. Not so early that you cause an unnecessary obstruction to faster moving traffic, but soon enough to give the novice plenty of time in which to find a safe gap. A new driver may need twice as long as a more experienced learner to prepare.

If someone is just about to overtake you, don't allow the pupil to signal if it is likely to cause this other driver to suddenly brake; allow them to being passing you first. But where the right-hand lane is full of traffic with no gap likely to arrive, tell your driver to signal early and then wait for a courteous person to open up a space for you. If they show hesitation in moving over when a gap does appear, be ready to urge them across as soon as it is safe as other motorists will not wait for long.

If the other drivers refuse to let you move across, or your pupil has missed a gap and you cannot find another one reasonably quickly, be careful! When this situation happens the learner may be so intent on watching for an opportunity to change lanes that they can forget to look where they are going. This could mean that the car will begin to drift off course or the driver will suddenly find that they have run out of road space. It is up to you to keep an eye on everything and prevent this kind of error.

Do NOT allow your pupil to twist around and look behind the car instead of using mirrors in this situation. There are occasions when a quick blind spot check might be appropriate, but if they start twisted around (as some do), they will almost certainly pull the wheel off course as they do so and they will not react in time if something brakes in front of them.

In future lessons, when your pupil is beginning to take more responsibility for their own actions, a small test will be to take them on to a dual carriageway, and without advising them of the type of road they are on, ask them to turn right. Not everyone will move to the right-hand lane in this case and one or two will position left-of-centre as if expecting oncoming traffic.

This incorrect positioning happened quite regularly with one ex-pupil of mine. She was not a complete novice, just forgetful! One day, I pulled her over and explained that the position she should have taken up on the approach to the last roundabout we went through was incorrect, and before driving on showed her (again) how the right turn position differed between dual carriageways and two-way roads. She nodded her understanding of the issue, set off again into two-way traffic, and when I asked her to turn right at the end of the street she smartly moved over to the wrong side of the road! Another car was entering our road at the top and flashed his lights as he saw us cross over the centre-line.

"Why is he doing that?" she enquired, *"Is he letting me go first?"* Back to the drawing board!

INTERSECTIONS

Intersections are perhaps the most troublesome aspect of dual carriageways, particularly when having to make a right turn from the main route into a side road where there will need to be a large reduction in speed and a lot of steering movement in a short space of time.

With a learner, if you ask them to turn right at the next intersection the chances are you will end up doing a U turn. If you want the pupil to turn off from the main carriageway into a side road on the right, you should stop and give a short briefing (Fig. 19).

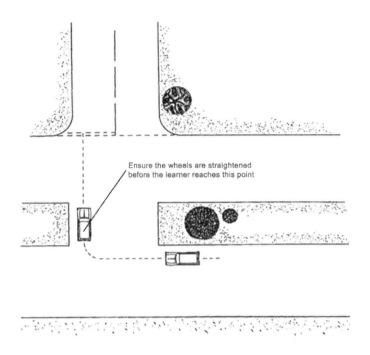

Figure 19. Turning right from a dual carriageway

It must be made clear that your intention is to cross the central reserve through the gap in order to reach the side road on the right. You must describe the relevant position to be taken up within the intersection, which in the absence of any road markings is normally well to the left. Explain that if the pupil were to use the right-hand side of the gap, and another vehicle entered the area, it would be forced to pull up on your left and as a result your view of the road would be blocked. To be on the safe side, ensure your trainee understands that they must give way to traffic coming from their left before crossing into the side road. Another important point to bring to your driver's attention is with regard to steering. As they enter the gap they should attempt to straighten the wheels as much as possible, especially if you have to stop. If this is not done, the novice will forget that the wheels are turned to the right, and when setting off you will end up 'swan necking' rather than heading in a straight line. Also, if you do have to wait in the central reserve while traffic passes, switch off the right-turn signal. From there you are in fact, going straight on into the side road and a continuing signal may mislead others into thinking you intend to complete a U turn.

When putting theory into practise, the most likely problem to occur is approaching too fast; failing to anticipate how much steering needs to be done catches many learners out. Ensure you get them to slow down properly before entering the gap.

Turning right on to a dual carriageway creates a whole new set of possibilities for error, both for new and experienced drivers alike and not everyone knows how to do it correctly.

Where a driver approaches from a side road and the intersection lies directly in front, turning right through the gap should be straightforward. With a pupil new to this type of junction though, be sure to stop first and brief them on what they need to do. Failure to do this could run the risk of a novice turning directly onto the wrong side of the road. You must act very quickly to pull the steering over if this happens.

This comparatively easy right turn may be complicated by the presence of another vehicle. If you have to stop at the end of the side road, and while you are waiting to cross to the middle another car enters the intersection indicating to the right, the question is; does the other driver wish to enter your road or complete a U turn? Many neglect to cancel the signal when they want to go straight on from the central reserve and the only safe solution is to instruct your pupil to wait and see what the other driver does. In this situation, the intersection should be regarded as part of the major road, so any vehicle emerging from the gap must be given priority. You should only venture forward with your learner when you are certain the other driver is coming straight on or they have cleared the area.

Most mistakes are made when the intersection lies to the left of your approach road (Fig. 20). Normally a compulsory left-turn sign will be seen on the approach; but you wish to turn right, so what would you do?

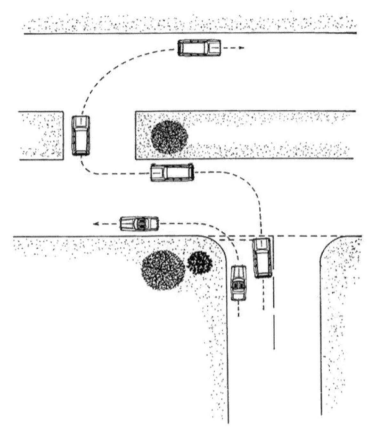

Figure 20. Turning right onto a dual carriageway where the intersection is offset to the left of the approach road

Despite the obvious necessity to turn left when emerging, a position nearer to the centre line should be taken up, and a signal to the right needs to be given just as you set off.

What should be done when the road you want to reach lies opposite the one you are on, and again the intersection is to the left of your approach? (Fig. 21).

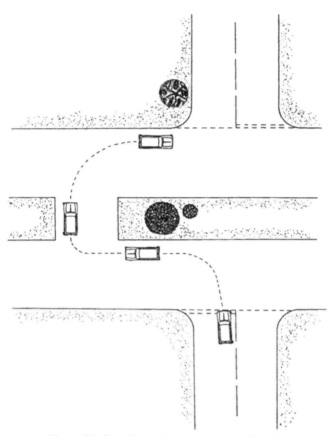

Figure 21. Crossing a dual carriageway where the intersection is offset to the left of the approach road

The approach from the side road into the central reserve should be carried out as for a right turn. Once within the gap the signal should be cancelled until you begin emerging, when a left turn signal needs to be given. This early signal makes it clear that you do not intend to stay on the main carriageway.

DUAL CARRIAGEWAYS AND THE NATIONAL SPEED LIMIT

If there is a fast stretch of dual carriageway in your locality, teach your learner how to make use of it once they have shown an ability to make good progress and have learned to judge speed accurately. A driving test candidate will be expected to show an ability to drive under varying road and traffic conditions and may be taken on such a road if one is within reach of a test route.

Driving tests apart, experience of fast moving traffic for the learner will stand them in good stead for any future motorway driving.

Learner drivers were banned from using motorways until a change of law in June 2018, when they were allowed onto them providing they were accompanied by an ADI in a car with dual controls. I have absolutely no idea what use the 'powers that be' think dual controls will be. If a learner loses control or makes a dangerous lane change on a motorway, stepping on a dual brake will only make the situation more dangerous; but unless you have this extra control you must stick to normal dual carriageways.

On a high-speed dual carriageway you will find cyclists and other slow moving vehicles, roundabouts, crossroads and intersections, and a lay-by here and there from which traffic may be emerging at low speed because there is no acceleration lane... a lot to deal with at fast speeds. There is also the danger of a broken down vehicle being left on the nearside lane due to the lack of a hard shoulder. A motorway has none of these problems, and usually has multiple lanes to keep traffic flowing more easily. Between the two the motorway is an easier and safer place to drive, and therefore a better road on which to introduce an inexperienced person to 70 mph motoring, but you and your pupil will not be allowed there.

Before taking your student driver into this new world of high-speed motoring, it is essential to equip them with the basic rules, most of which can be found within the Highway Code and Driving manual. I would highly recommend that you refresh your knowledge here before venturing out.

There are, however, a few extra points to be made. When picking up speed in the acceleration lane, you do not necessarily have to push the learner to 70 mph, but they must reach a minimum of 50-60 mph if they are to avoid causing hindrance to traffic already on the carriageway.

Another important point to explain is the need for blind spot checks before moving out onto the main carriageway, many people neglect this and use only the mirrors, this is NOT acceptable. The blind spot which exists when moving off from the kerbside does not disappear when you are on the move, and is quite possible for a vehicle to be in another lane on your right which cannot be seen in the mirrors. Tell your pupil that when this is done they must be careful to avoid twisting round in the seat and pulling the steering wheel over.

On the carriageway itself, two main points need to be hammered home; keeping a safe distance from any vehicles in front (at *least* a two-second gap in good conditions) and plenty of mirror-work. The driver must be aware of what is behind and what other vehicles are doing at all times. The only way to find out if they are aware is to question them; ask what they can see and what they think is likely to happen.

When you intend to leave the carriageway, inform your pupil in advance that they should avoid reducing speed after signalling as they normally would, but to wait until they have entered the slip road or deceleration lane before slowing down. Sometimes the brakes will have to be used quite firmly if the deceleration lane is short, and your pupil should also be made aware of this well before you get there.

At the exit, ensure the left-turn signal is given in good time; many people leave the indication until they are on top of the slip road, which gives virtually no warning at all and can be infuriating for the driver behind if they have just pulled out needlessly to overtake you. Once within the slip road you will almost certainly have to remind the pupil to switch off the signal.

If you have no high-speed dual carriageway within easy reach, I would recommend that you make the effort at some stage to take your trainee on a longer drive in order to practise on one, even if this is after they have passed the driving test.

After passing the test you should certainly endeavour to get the pupil out on to the motorway for some training. One of my other books, *'The Glovebox Guide to Motorway Driving'* available in paperback and on Kindle, could be a useful source of reference for this training.

ANIMALS, CHILDREN AND THE LEARNER

We all know what a nuisance stray animals can be when they wander into your path, and with a learner behind the wheel you must be twice as wary. If this happens, the novice's natural instincts will be to stamp on the brakes in an all-out emergency stop; this must be prevented. The only way of doing this is to constantly scan your surroundings so that in the event of a problem being spotted; the pupil can be given early warning to slow down.

Most learners tend only to notice what lies directly in front of them until a movement at the side suddenly catches their attention. You need to be twice as observant to make up for this. You must be able to prepare a beginner for things like children running into the road well before the need to take action arises. When possible danger is seen, instruct your pupil to check the mirrors to see what is behind and then get them to slow down, covering the brake if need be until the hazard is passed.

Children can be very unpredictable, and sometimes will deliberately step out in front of a learner. Unless they are obviously aware of your presence and moving out of the way, instruct your pupil to give a light tap on the horn to let them know you are there. Once you have their attention, a smile and a wave of thanks will hopefully prevent them from reacting in a negative way to the warning.

MAJOR CROSSROADS

Tackling a right turn at a busy crossroads can be a daunting prospect for the learner driver. In addition to things they have previously encountered when turning right, they will have to deal with the possibility of more oncoming traffic, a greater number of vehicles waiting behind, other cars turning right across your path, and the presence of traffic lights, with or without filter lights and lanes.

Crossroads are anything but a standard design. In your own experience you will have come across a great many varieties: different light and lane set-ups, staggered or angled roads, 'offside' or 'nearside' turns, some with road markings of varying design and some without, confusing isn't it?

An experienced motorist can feel their way through an unfamiliar junction whereas a learner needs more time to think and act. Even if your pupil has been taken through these crossroads many times as a passenger, there is no guarantee that they will know what to do. Things can look very different from the driving seat; and let's face it; most kids these days when they're travelling have their attention on nothing other than their mobile phones!

A detailed explanation of how to approach this type of junction needs to be given. Stop, if possible, within sight of the first one you intend to go through. Point out the differences between nearside and offside turning with regard to positioning of the car on approach, and mention the advantage and disadvantage of each.

Offside Turning

The offside turn (Fig. 22) gives a better view of any oncoming traffic , but makes steering more difficult. It also restricts the number of vehicles that can make the turn compared to nearside turning. I cannot remember the last time I made an offside turn at a crossroads; the sheer volume of traffic on most roads makes this impractical and most drivers will automatically make the nearside turn instead. I would still make your pupil aware of this method however just in case the need arises.

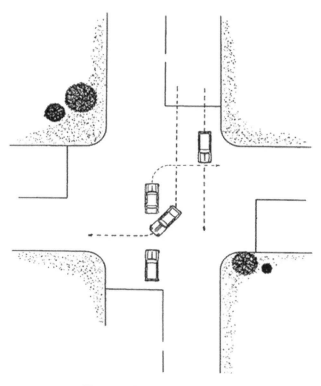

Figure 22. Turning offside to offside

Nearside Turning

The nearside turn means that the view of oncoming traffic may be blocked, but makes it easier for a continuous stream of right-turning drivers to pass through.

At a crossroads where oncoming traffic is also turning right, instruct your pupil to move forward when the lights are in your favour and to watch the position of the leading vehicle opposite. If the driver begins turning in front of your car give the order to stop (if necessary) and wait for a safe gap. From this position you can then turn using the nearside method but you must keep your car parallel while waiting (Fig.23)

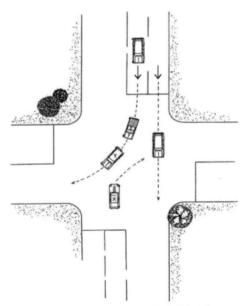

Figure 23. Cars Y and Z caused car X to hold back for a nearside to nearside turn. Car X must wait in a parallel position as traffic may still come straight on from both opposing lanes

Copying the other drivers, which beginners are likely to do, and moving into a partly turned position, could obstruct oncoming traffic (Fig. 24).

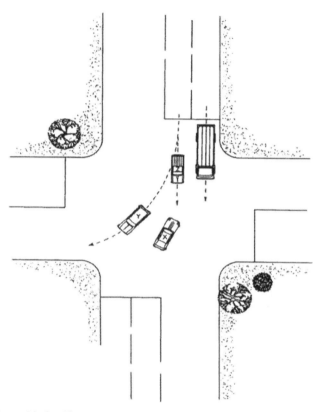

Figure 24. Car Y turned using the nearside method which car X copied, but car X made the mistake of waiting in an angled position blocking the path of oncoming driver Z

The nearside turn is generally easier to carry out than the offside one and it is certainly far more commonly used. Many crossroads are now marked or made wider to provide an extra lane for this purpose. Some junctions are therefore very clearly marked but, remember, learners rarely notice road markings unless they are pointed out as they are usually too busy staring at other traffic.

Before attempting a nearside turn, show the pupil the type of markings that may be found on the road. Where there is a designated right turn lane, and the junction is wide enough, then it will be okay to wait in the half turned position (Fig.25).

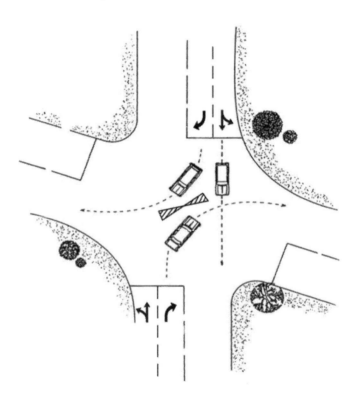

Figure 25. Using a dedicated right turn lane at a crossroads

At some traffic light junctions, a right turn filter may show first, in which case it is imperative that the trainee is forewarned that if the filter goes out and red and amber shows, the lights are about to change to normal green. In this case inform them that they should carry on if it is safe but that they must be prepared to stop and give way to oncoming traffic.

The danger of the nearside turn is that oncoming traffic can be hidden from view, even when there is only one vehicle turning across your path. This is where good observation is critical; make the pupil aware of the danger. A low speed must be maintained until you can see clearly past other vehicles.

It may be that at a fairly busy crossroads, an opportunity to complete the turn does not arise until the lights change and oncoming traffic is halted. When this happens, as you well know, there is only one thing to do - move off quickly to clear the junction. This is another thing the learner will need to know in advance. Advise them that while they are waiting in the middle, in addition to looking for a gap in the traffic, they must also keep a check on the lights, and if they do start changing they must be ready to move as soon as it is safe. Without prior warning of things like this the pupil is almost certain to panic and this usually results in stalling. While a stall is not a major disaster, doing it in the middle of a major crossroads is not ideal!

In future, if you decide to turn at a junction similar to the previous one you need only remind your pupil of what to do on the approach. But where a different set up is encountered, stop again for a proper briefing before attempting it.

When the pupil has gained some experience and is starting to make decisions without your guidance, they can be let off the reins at a crossroads to see what approach they will use. Allowing them to use their own initiative at some point is essential in preparing the driver for the test and subsequent solo driving.

6
PLANNING A LESSON PROGRAMME

Teaching someone the skill of driving is no easy occupation. It can be made a little easier, though, when you have a basic plan in mind, one which teaches the student certain things before going on to anything more demanding. This way the pupil will progress more easily and your work can be less of a strain.

A trainee cannot be programmed like a computer, however. We cannot simply say that they should be taught how to do an emergency stop on the fifth lesson and how to reverse on the seventh, it doesn't work like that. Some people need more time to practise on certain areas than others. Although every learner begins at about the same level and reaches the same goal, the journey each one takes will be along a different road. These roads may run roughly parallel but they do not all have the same length. And some have more hills than others!

Each novice an instructor takes on is an individual and has to be treated as such, and the sequence of subjects a new driver is taught can sometimes depend on the area from which they begin their lessons. A pupil being picked up in a city centre can hardly be expected to tackle extremely busy roundabouts after just a few hours of junction practise, whereas someone starting from the quiet outskirts of town could probably practise on roundabouts in their local area at an early stage.

What you should aim for is a fairly systematic approach, but this must be tailored when the need arises to suit the individual or the area in which you are teaching. For example, a beginner who lives in a city centre region may be taken into a quiet back street area to be taught the basic skills of car control and junction work, but after several hours of this, if things have gone according to plan, you will both want to move on. The next step would normally be approaching roundabouts, but if those nearby are very busy it would be extremely unwise to throw a novice into this while trying to teach a new skill.

There are two ways around this problem. One is to continue practising in the quiet area but introduce something new such as the emergency stop, or begin laying down the foundations of reversing. This way the pupil is still making progress and is able to gain sound experience in car control before venturing into traffic. The other solution is to drive the beginner to another area during the lesson, or simply to start the tuition in a different locality where quiet roundabouts can be found.

Whichever way you decide to go about your training, there is a rule to follow if the teaching is to stand any real chance of success; things must be done logically. There is little point expecting a pupil to do a turn in the road, for example, before they have been taught how to reverse. And asking a novice to reverse around a corner before they have the ability to control the car in a straight line is hardly common sense. I have already pointed out that everyone cannot be taught in exactly the same way, but certain things must be covered with the pupil before expecting them to move on to other exercises. There can be no definite order of events but some things must be taught before others.

Starting a driver off is the most straightforward part - everyone must first be taught moving off and stopping followed by gear changing. Naturally, the next main step is junctions, but before this, clutch control should be covered.

As mentioned in Chapter 3, the skill of controlling the clutch is required to have full control over junction work, but apart from this, it is probably the most difficult aspect of car control for a novice to master. This is one skill which needs to be introduced early. A driver needs control over the clutch when moving off, especially at an angle or uphill. It must be mastered before any manoeuvre can successfully be attempted. When stopping, it may be necessary to use clutch control to edge into a more convenient position. Driving in slow moving traffic demands a good command over the clutch to avoid those 'kangaroo starts' and nervous jerks and stalls. Some people will need a lot of practise before they can really get the feel of the clutch so the sooner this is worked on the better.

With junctions themselves the old adage about not trying to run before you can walk should be followed. Some instructors encourage beginners to carry on at each give way even at the very start of junction work. A few will maybe handle this, but most will be pushed into making unnecessary mistakes, and this practise hardly develops sound observation techniques in the pupil. Most of the observation has to be done by the instructor while the learner concentrates on the controls. The novice will then grow to think that proper observation is done as an afterthought rather than as a priority. The three-stage principle of junction practice works well and teaches a pupil the importance of correct speed and observation on the approach.

1. Stop at all junctions initially (unless to do so would confuse following traffic).
2. After some progress is seen begin to drive on where a good safe view can be obtained but continue to halt where vision is restricted.
3. Finally, after mastering the clutch, you can urge your pupil to drive on at all junctions where safe and correct to do so.

Instructing in this manner will teach the learner to treat junctions with the respect and caution they deserve.

Traffic lights, pedestrian crossings and such like should be avoided until you are sure the pupil can move off and stop without difficulty, and they must also be reasonably conversant with the use and changing of gears before being taken out into any traffic. In some areas these everyday hazards will be almost impossible to avoid without driving round in circles, but try not to lead your pupil at the novice stage into areas where they will be put under undue pressure. A gradual introduction of these routine obstacles is best so that they can learn to deal with each in turn rather than being inundated with everything at once the first time they drive into traffic.

To introduce the learner to busier roads, while you are practising in quiet areas, if the pupil seems settled and capable enough, take them out into a little traffic for a short while to broaden their experience but return to a quieter place to give them time to relax and allow things to sink in. With this gradual introduction to other hazards and busier roads, the transition to heavy traffic can be made eventually without the trainee thinking they have crossed some kind of boundary where things suddenly become dangerous!

Having shown an ability to control the car during normal driving operations, providing there are no obvious weaknesses the pupil can be moved on to the next objectives - the set manoeuvres. Angle starts and hill starts may already have been done to some degree and can be polished up, then you can progress to the more demanding exercises.

The emergency stop should be taught first I believe as it increases the pupil's confidence in their use of the brakes; a skill which could come in useful when you are starting to mix with other road users! It will help alleviate fears the novice may have about having to brake firmly at lights, for instance, and if a real emergency arises during a lesson there is less chance of the pupil panic braking, or worse still, failing to brake at all.

Logic dictates that the beginner is next taught how to reverse in a straight line, then around corners, and finally into parking bays and spaces. Only when reversing has been well practised should the more complicated turn in the road be attempted; an exercise that is probably the ultimate test of a learner's control over the machine.

The turn combines practically every skill a driver needs in car control. They must be able to turn the steering quickly and at the same time keep the speed under slow control. They must combine the clutch, gas and parking brake when starting off on a cambered road and then control the speed of the car when it begins to roll down the slope. They must have reversing ability and be able to carry out safe all-round observation while all this is going on. So, obviously, all the skills required for the exercise have to be taught and practised before the turn itself can be tried.

Having completed all the manoeuvres, a learner will normally be able to spend more time out in traffic learning to cope with all the fun and games that come along with it, though some beginners who get stuck and experience difficulties with reversing and turns in the road may find that their whole driving ability suffers as a result of lost confidence. When this happens, and it is not by any means rare, you will need to take a step back and give extra tuition on subjects already covered in order to regain a previous standard before pushing things along again. But generally by now, the learner driver will be capable of venturing into gradually busier areas and tackling the awkward junctions which before you sought to avoid.

As you develop the pupil's ability and encounter all the various types of junctions and road layouts, along with heavier traffic, you should aim to make the lessons as varied as possible. It is no good following the same route each time, just allowing them to drive to work and back, for instance. Although this may help a little it will become routine and doesn't offer much of a challenge or sustain the driver's interest. Wide experience and practise are what is needed to pass a driving test and this is what you must endeavour to give your student.

On each lesson you should practise whichever manoeuvres have been taught; and also try to include a little of everything else... a few roundabouts, a stretch of dual carriageway, roads of differing speed limits, busy main routes and some quiet back streets with those blind corners and narrow spaces. This is the sort of thing a driver can expect when taking the test. Each route will cover a variety of roads to test the candidate's ability to get about safely under varying traffic conditions.

As you go from lesson to lesson, any subject which was introduced on a previous session must be re-capped and practised before moving on to anything new. This is the only way to ensure your pupil continues where they left off, otherwise they will easily forget past advice and only be able to cope with the new.

When a particular weakness has shown up during a drive, concentrate on it until improvement is seen in order to keep every aspect of the trainee's driving to a similar standard. Any weakness left uncorrected is likely to be where a test candidate's driving suffers most when they are under stress... a potential failure point.

7
DEVELOPING RESPONSIBILITY

As a pupil's ability and experience develop, there comes a time when they must be weaned and made into a driver who is capable of making their own decisions and carrying them out safely. There is not much point in constantly coaching the pupil all the way through every lesson and then abandoning them to their own resources when they take a driving test. They must become largely independent before this time to stand any chance of passing.

The transition from novice stage to test standard driving has to be brought about gradually; there are no clear cut borderlines between each level. This can only be accomplished by a skilled instructor who gets to know the capabilities of each student and keeps quiet when things are going along nicely, but is always ready to step in with a word of advice or encouragement when something out of the ordinary crops up or the pupil appears uncertain of what to do.

Where does this process begin? At an early stage most novices will begin to make simple decisions for themselves such as when to change gear. After repeated instruction on basic skills such as this, it should only be a short while before the pupil anticipates the need to make a change up to a higher gear. You need not then give an instruction if they appear ready to go ahead on their own and are capable of doing so.

For a less co-ordinated or nervous driver however, who may be reluctant to do anything without a word from you, some encouragement must be given. If you consider it time that they were able to change gear on their own, stop the car and suggest this. Show them the approximate speeds at which to use each gear as a guideline, and then at least allow them to attempt changing up without help, though do give assistance if problems develop during an effort at this. But when approaching hazards when timing is more important, a reminder of which gear to select and when to change down would be appropriate until a little more competence is achieved in this area.

Another situation where the novice can be given a little responsibility at a fairly basic stage is when moving off or stopping. Signals are not an obvious necessity when no one is there to see them. Ensure your pupil understands this, and when you intend to make a stop, inform the driver of where you want them to park, and then instruct them to check the mirrors, and tell them to give a signal 'if necessary', and see if they make the right decision.

Having shown an ability to carry out this simple exercise easily enough then give a little more leeway. Simply ask your student to find a convenient parking place on the left, leaving them to consider whether a signal is required, if so when to give it, and also to test their choice of a safe stopping place. If they stop in what is not the most convenient place, explain why and suggest a more suitable position. This way they will be taught to think before acting in future, a process sadly missing in many everyday drivers.

The routine of approaching junctions is probably the next thing learners will begin to take upon themselves. When your driver shows signs of starting the necessary actions before your prompting, allow them to continue unaided if what they are doing is correct; on the final run-up though it still has to be up to you to ensure correct speed for the conditions. When to emerge is your decision alone until the pupil gains a reasonable amount of experience.

The manoeuvres are another subject where, unless the driver is experiencing problems, you should soon be able to let them carry out the mechanics of the exercises without continuous instruction. But as with junctions, when other road users become affected by your movements, step in to guide the novice, as much to keep them from becoming flustered as for any other reason. Once they have established good control over the car they can then be allowed to start dealing with other road users themselves.

For instance, after practising reversing regularly and encountering traffic coming from different directions, you will have instructed them on what to do in each case. When similar occurrences crop up you may then wait to see if they notice and react to the presence of other people, but step in yourself if they are late to respond in order to keep things safe.

Allowing a learner to gradually take control over their own actions is the only real way of telling whether the tuition has been absorbed. When you are sure they can do things such as a turn in the road without help from you, and keep full control over the car even when other people are waiting and watching, you can be confident that things are going well.

Out on the open road matters have to be approached a little more carefully. It would obviously be unwise to let a beginner with only limited experience run riot in busy traffic. The surrendering of your control must begin in quieter areas where you can be sure a wrong move by the pupil will not cause any real danger. Let us begin the process with a fairly new driver who has spent several hours driving in light traffic... Previously you have been giving almost total instruction. The pupil may be changing gear on their own but you have been pointing out all the hazards and instructing your driver safely past them. Before you can give the pupil real responsibility, no matter on how small a level, you must establish whether or not they are beginning to read the road. Question them; ask what they see ahead and to the sides. Often the reply will indicate that they are not thinking very far ahead and this will need improvement before they can start planning their own drive. Work on this if need be until, when they are quizzed as to what lies ahead, their answers pick out the hazards you are concerned about.

As you approach traffic lights the driver at this stage should be familiar with what to do but ensure the mirrors are used well in advance (mirror-work must be hammered home until it is second nature). And where two or more lanes may be used for going straight on, ask the pupil which lane should be used. A common mistake at lights is approaching in a left-hand lane which is obviously blocked just after the junction. If the lights force you to stop, the driver is then left with the difficult task of struggling through the build up of traffic into the next lane. Once a beginner spots a hazard such as traffic lights, they usually fails to see anything beyond the stop line until actually crossing it. Your pupil should be questioned early enough in this situation so that you have time to make a lane change comfortably when you have had to point out an obstruction that the driver has failed to mention. When the time comes for a lane change, instruct the trainee to check mirrors, give them the option of whether to signal or not, and at this stage tell them when to move out, or when not to!

Another failing of learner drivers (and many experienced drivers), is in noticing road signs. As part of my work I have taken many people for advanced training and as a test of observation I often ask, *"What was the last warning sign you saw? "* Even though it may have only been seconds past, not very many could answer correctly or even remembered seeing one! If these are advanced drivers, what hope can we have for our learners?

Encourage them from the outset to take notice of road signs, in particular signs of warning. Include observation checks as part of your training programme. When a driver is questioned as to what they can see ahead, they might mention a cyclist and a parked car or two, but for some reason an obvious warning sign goes unheeded. Bring their attention to it and ask what it means. You may also do a similar test when joining a new road; ask what the speed limit is, there may have been signs indicating a change.

As the pupil nears the intermediate stage, junctions should by now be a routine task. Turns into minor roads may be completely in their own hands, except where you need to give advice; perhaps when pedestrians are crossing the road or to warn of the possible or actual approach of traffic when the mouth of the junction is narrowed by parked cars. Particular care needs to be taken, though, when entering a side turning where the view is restricted; a new driver will only react to things which are visible. Your job here is to teach anticipation and to warn the trainee of what might be hidden around the corner and what action may have to be taken.

So now we are at the stage where the pupil can manage to control the vehicle without too much help from you, and they are beginning to make fairly simple decisions. There will still be times when plenty of instruction is required from you as situations new to the driver appear, especially as you venture into busier traffic or if your driver is lacking in confidence. But where a trainee is well versed in a particular area be careful not to over-instruct, you must allow them room to develop.

The transition from intermediate pupil to test standard is just as gradual. You will eventually reach a position where the learner will start to make major decisions in addition to the smaller ones. Though this must only be allowed when you are sure the driver has mastered mirror work and can show a sound judgement of speed and distance.

Junctions may also be taken a step further. When joining a major road, make sure the driver is looking early enough and instruct them to drive on if the way is clear. They can choose their own gap but it may be a wise plan to be ready with the parking brake unless you are sure there is no danger, a relatively inexperienced pupil isn't always going to make the right decision. The most common fault is failing to judge correctly the speed of oncoming traffic. Sometimes two-wheelers may be missed; in being so concerned about cars and lorries these smaller vehicles can go unnoticed.

way of preventing these mistakes is to get your driver ch slowly enough. Not at crawling speed; except for ⌐lind junctions, but slow enough to be able to look carefully and take everything in; a priority which should have been pressed home when the novice was first taught how to emerge from junctions. Even when the speed has been brought down enough though, there is no guarantee of things going according to plan. A nervous driver is often more concerned with people who may be waiting behind and could be in too much of a hurry to move on. Always be ready to take control of the situation.

As a pupil's road reading improves, observation checks can become more discreet. For instance, when approaching a dual-carriageway with a mandatory left turn sign at the junction, rather than pointing out the sign, simply direct the driver to follow the signs. With a more advanced student you need not say anything at all.

As a more demanding test for an experienced pupil, take them into a one-way system if possible and leave them to find their own way through, unless a certain lane needs to be taken up for your destination. You could direct them to move over to the appropriate lane and then ask them to follow the road markings. To expand on this, when in a fairly quiet area, if road markings are clearly shown just ask your pupil to follow the lane indicating, say, the city centre. The question is; will the driver go through the proper routine of checking mirrors, finding a safe gap, indicating where necessary, and then selecting the correct lane, or will they be too occupied with looking for clues on the road? If everything is done safely, you have a pupil nearing readiness for test. If not, give extra tuition in this area then check their ability again with a similar test.

Other problems you can set for an advanced pupil include reaction to no-entry signs. Choose a place where there are two roads reasonably close together, with the first displaying a no-entry or no vehicles sign. Tell your driver that you want them to take the next available road on the right, or left, whichever is the case. Most will make the obvious error of preparing to turn into the no-entry the first time you try this, so don't attempt it on a busy road or when there are other vehicles following close behind. Naturally, you must not actually allow them to make the turn; the mistake will be evident early enough for you to correct the situation.

A final test for the pupil's sign reading skills is in asking them to carry on to a set destination with only the information signs and road markings at junctions to guide them. Approaching a roundabout say, tell them to take the exit marked for the A45 and then to follow the outer ring road. If they can choose the correct route, while keeping full safe control over the vehicle, they are sure to be nearing test standard and independent driving.

'Independent driving' is now a part of the driving test. At some point during the test, a candidate will either be asked to follow a series of traffic signs, or they will have to follow 'sat nav' directions for around 20 minutes. Knowing how to interpret the directions from a sat nav is very important, and once your pupil has reached a stage of independence you need to make sure that they get plenty of practise doing this. It is important that they can do this confidently and without assistance. If a driver lacks this bit of extra polish their chances of being successful the first time the test is taken are fairly remote.

Many instructors have average or poor pass rates simply because they do not insist on those extra few hours which are needed to boost a pupil's confidence and gain more experience. Some of them don't even bother with a sat nav! They make the mistake of bringing the novice to the basic level of driving skill they deem to be sufficient before submitting them for test. The drawback is, even the best driver's ability will suffer from examination nerves and without that extra polish the final standard is unlikely to be good enough.

The story should be different, however, if the candidate has those extra lessons under their belt. They will of course make mistakes, all drivers do on test, but hopefully they will be able to demonstrate to the examiner that even when they are not at their best they can still manage to get about safely. They can also show that enough experience has been gained to be able to cope with the everyday stress and strain of driving. Before taking your student for test you must satisfy yourself of certain things:

- Can the pupil carry out all the requirements of the test without the need of help from you?
- Do they have the confidence in their own ability to be able to make decisions without looking to you for assistance?
- Can they continue to drive to the standard they have reached while under the pressure of the driving test?

The first two conditions can be answered by a competent trainer, but the third will remain a mystery unless you can do something to simulate the conditions the pupil is likely to expect on the driving test. This is where the importance of a mock test comes in. A mock test is a very good idea for two reasons;

1. It will demonstrate to the pupil what to expect on the day, leaving them more prepared; half the reason for test nerves is fear of the unknown.
2. It will prove whether your learner has, in fact, mastered the skills they have been taught and whether or not they are indeed, ready for test.

The best way to go about this would be to ask a local driving school to conduct a mock test on your behalf. This would really give a much more accurate assessment than trying to do it yourself. The driver would understandably be nervous of the stranger (further simulating a test situation) and, in addition, a professional opinion on the pupil's ability may certainly be worth having at this stage. As mentioned at the start of this book however, do make sure you choose a decent instructor to carry this out for you!

If you do this, I would strongly recommend that you sit in the back of the car during the drive. You may be surprised at some of the things a normally competent driver will do when under pressure.

After the test you can sit back and discuss the drive, pick out the parts which were shown to be weak and work out between the two of you whether the pupil is ready for the real thing. You may decide to fit in extra lessons to work on any faults which were evident or even postpone the test for a while if the drive was of poor standard.

The test should not be applied for until the pupil is ready. Some driving schools insist on pupils sending in application forms almost as soon as they have a provisional licence. The official excuse for doing this is that it gives the pupil something to work towards (the unofficial reason is that it in some way ties the pupil to the school which booked the test for them and discourages them from going elsewhere for lessons). Either way it is unnecessary and wrong. To give a novice driver a deadline to work to only puts them under pressure. If you have made the mistake of applying for a test appointment too early, and the mock test shows the pupil to be unready... postpone! Your trainee may argue against the decision to postpone and want to take the test anyway. You must not give in and let them 'have a go.' They are almost certain to fail and may do so quite badly, leading to shattered confidence.

If all does go well and your learner is shown to be ready for test, now is the time to apply if you have not already done so; the easiest way to do this is through the DVSA website.

It is round about this time that the pupil may start to worry needlessly about the silly stories they often hear. These are generally absolute rubbish, put about either by cowboy instructors trying to make excuses for their poor pass rates, or by individual test candidates who haven't the strength of character to admit they were just not good enough on the day.

It is up to you to provide confidence where it may be lacking, and to explain that the test is not the great ordeal it is made out to be, but just another drive with a stranger as a passenger, and perhaps a reward at the end.

Printed in Great Britain
by Amazon